Favorite Brand Name™

All-New

Low-Carb
Recipes

Publications International, Ltd.
Favorite Brand Name Recipes at www.fbnr.com

Nutritional Analysis: Linda R. Yoakam, M.S., R.D., L.D.

Pictured on the front cover: Smoked Salmon Roses *(page 30).*
Pictured on the back cover *(clockwise from top left):* Thai Broccoli Salad *(page 104),* Grilled Red Snapper with Avocado-Papaya Salsa *(page 148)* and Pineapple-Ginger Bavarian *(page 166).*

ISBN: 1-4127-2091-5

Library of Congress Control Number: 2004109273

Manufactured in China.

8 7 6 5 4 3 2 1

Nutritional Analysis: The nutritional information that appears with each recipe was submitted in part by the participating companies and associations. Every effort has been made to check the accuracy of these numbers. However, because numerous variables account for a wide range of values for certain foods, nutritive analyses in this book should be considered approximate.

Microwave Cooking: Microwave ovens vary in wattage. Use the cooking times as guidelines and check for doneness before adding more time.

Preparation/Cooking Times: Preparation times are based on the approximate amount of time required to assemble the recipe before cooking, baking, chilling or serving. These times include preparation steps such as measuring, chopping and mixing. The fact that some preparations and cooking can be done simultaneously is taken into account. Preparation of optional ingredients and serving suggestions is not included.

Note: This book is for informational purposes and is not intended to provide medical advice. Neither Publications International, Ltd., nor the authors, editors or publisher take responsibility for any possible consequences from any treatment, procedure, exercise, dietary modification, action, or applications of medication or preparation by any person reading or following the information in this cookbook. The publication of this book does not constitute the practice of medicine, and this cookbook does not attempt to replace your physician or your pharmacist. **Before undertaking any course of treatment, the authors, editors and publisher advise the reader to check with a physician or other health care provider.**

contents

hearty breakfasts

Swiss Canadian Bacon & Eggs

Makes 4 servings

 8 eggs
¼ cup milk
½ teaspoon salt
¼ teaspoon black pepper
⅓ cup finely chopped green onions, divided
　　Nonstick cooking spray
 4 slices Canadian bacon, cut in half
 1 cup (4 ounces) shredded Swiss cheese

1. Preheat broiler.

2. Whisk together eggs, milk, salt and pepper in medium bowl until well blended. Reserve 2 tablespoons green onions; stir remaining green onions into egg mixture.

3. Spray 12-inch ovenproof skillet with cooking spray; heat over medium-low heat until hot. Add egg mixture. Cover and cook 14 minutes or until almost set.

4. Arrange bacon in pinwheel on top of egg mixture. Sprinkle with cheese; broil 2 minutes or until cheese is bubbly. Top with reserved 2 tablespoons green onions. Cut into 4 wedges. Serve immediately.

nutrients per serving: 309 Calories, 4g Carbohydrate, <1g Dietary Fiber, 20g Total Fat, 9g Saturated Fat, 466mg Cholesterol, 892mg Sodium, 27g Protein

Swiss Canadian Bacon & Eggs

Blueberry Cheesecake Muffins

Makes 12 muffins

1 package (8 ounces) cream cheese, softened
1 cup plus 1 tablespoon no-calorie sugar substitute for baking,
    divided
2 eggs
1 teaspoon *each* grated lemon peel and vanilla
¾ cup bran flakes cereal
½ cup *each* all-purpose flour and soy flour
2 teaspoons baking powder
¼ teaspoon salt
¾ cup milk
3 tablespoons melted butter
4 tablespoons no-sugar-added blueberry fruit spread
½ teaspoon ground cinnamon

1. Preheat oven to 350°F. Spray 12 muffin cups with nonstick cooking spray.

2. Beat cream cheese, ¼ cup sugar substitute, 1 egg, lemon peel and vanilla in medium bowl until smooth.

3. Combine cereal, flours, ¼ cup sugar substitute, baking powder and salt in medium bowl. In separate small bowl, whisk milk, butter and remaining egg until blended; pour over cereal mixture. Mix gently just until blended.

4. Spoon about 2 tablespoons batter into each muffin cup; spread with 1 teaspoon fruit spread. Spread cream cheese mixture over fruit spread. Mix remaining 1 tablespoon sugar substitute and cinnamon; sprinkle over cream cheese mixture.

5. Bake 30 to 35 minutes or until toothpicks inserted into centers come out clean. Cool muffins 10 minutes in pan on wire rack. Remove muffins from pan and cool. Serve warm or at room temperature. Refrigerate leftover muffins.

nutrients per serving (1 muffin): **178** Calories, 14g Carbohydrate, 1g Dietary Fiber, 11g Total Fat, 6g Saturated Fat, 66mg Cholesterol, 247mg Sodium, 5g Protein

Blueberry Cheesecake Muffins

Zucchini Mushroom Frittata

Makes 6 servings

1½ cups EGG BEATERS®
½ cup (2 ounces) shredded reduced-fat Swiss cheese
¼ cup fat-free (skim) milk
½ teaspoon garlic powder
¼ teaspoon seasoned pepper
  Nonstick cooking spray
1 medium zucchini, shredded (1 cup)
1 medium tomato, chopped
1 (4-ounce) can sliced mushrooms, drained
  Tomato slices and fresh basil leaves, for garnish

In medium bowl, combine Egg Beaters®, cheese, milk, garlic powder and seasoned pepper; set aside.

Spray 10-inch ovenproof nonstick skillet lightly with nonstick cooking spray. Over medium-high heat, sauté zucchini, tomato and mushrooms in skillet until tender. Pour egg mixture into skillet, stirring well. Cover; cook over low heat for 15 minutes or until cooked on bottom and almost set on top. Remove lid and place skillet under broiler for 2 to 3 minutes or until desired doneness. Slide onto serving platter; cut into wedges to serve. Garnish with tomato slices and basil.

Prep Time: 20 minutes
Cook Time: 20 minutes

nutrients per serving (1 frittata wedge (⅙ of total recipe) without garnish): 70 Calories, 5g Carbohydrate, 1g Dietary Fiber, 1g Total Fat, 1g Saturated Fat, 5mg Cholesterol, 316mg Sodium, 9g Protein

Zucchini Mushroom Frittata

Sun-Dried Tomato Scones

Makes 1½ dozen scones

  2 cups buttermilk baking mix
  ¼ cup (1 ounce) grated Parmesan cheese
1½ teaspoons dried basil leaves
  ⅔ cup reduced-fat (2%) milk
  ½ cup chopped drained oil-packed sun-dried tomatoes
  ¼ cup chopped green onions

Preheat oven to 450°F. Mix baking mix, cheese and basil in bowl. Stir in milk, tomatoes and onions. Mix just until dry ingredients are moistened. Drop by heaping teaspoonfuls onto greased baking sheet. Bake 8 to 10 minutes or until golden.

nutrients per serving (1 scone): 75 Calories, 10g Carbohydrate, <1g Dietary Fiber, 3g Total Fat, <1g Saturated Fat, 2mg Cholesterol, 209mg Sodium, 2g Protein

Country Ham Omelets

Makes 4 servings

  2 tablespoons butter or margarine
  3 slices HILLSHIRE FARM® Ham, chopped
  ½ cup finely chopped potato
  ¼ cup *each* chopped green bell pepper and chopped onion
  ½ cup sliced fresh mushrooms
  8 to 12 eggs, beaten
  ½ cup (2 ounces) shredded sharp Cheddar cheese

Melt butter in medium skillet over medium heat; sauté Ham, potato, pepper and onion 3 to 4 minutes. Add mushrooms; stir and heat through. Prepare four 2 or 3 egg omelets. Fill each with 2 tablespoons cheese and ¼ cup ham mixture. Use remaining ham mixture as omelet topping.

nutrients per serving: 292 Calories, 7g Carbohydrate, 1g Dietary Fiber, 21g Total Fat, 10g Saturated Fat, 459mg Cholesterol, 352mg Sodium, 18g Protein

Sun-Dried Tomato Scones

Greek Isles Omelet

Makes 2 servings

Nonstick cooking spray
¼ cup chopped onion
¼ cup canned artichoke hearts, rinsed and drained
¼ cup washed and torn spinach leaves
¼ cup chopped plum tomato
1 cup cholesterol-free egg substitute
2 tablespoons sliced pitted ripe olives, rinsed and drained
Dash black pepper

1. Spray small nonstick skillet with cooking spray; heat over medium heat until hot. Cook and stir onion 2 minutes or until crisp-tender.

2. Add artichoke hearts. Cook and stir until heated through. Add spinach and tomato; toss briefly. Remove from heat. Transfer vegetables to small bowl. Wipe out skillet and spray with cooking spray.

3. Combine egg substitute, olives and pepper in medium bowl. Heat skillet over medium heat until hot. Pour egg mixture into skillet. Cook over medium heat 5 to 7 minutes; as eggs begin to set, gently lift edge of omelet with spatula and tilt skillet so uncooked portion flows underneath.

4. When egg mixture is set, spoon vegetable mixture over half of omelet. Loosen omelet with spatula and fold in half. Slide omelet onto serving plate.

nutrients per serving (½ of omelet): **111 Calories, 7g Carbohydrate, 1g Dietary Fiber, 3g Total Fat, <1g Saturated Fat, 0mg Cholesterol, 538mg Sodium, 13g Protein**

Greek Isles Omelet

Ham & Cheddar Frittata

Makes 4 servings

 3 eggs
 3 egg whites
 ½ teaspoon salt
 ½ teaspoon freshly ground black pepper
 1½ cups (4 ounces) frozen broccoli florets, thawed
 6 ounces deli smoked ham, cut into ½-inch cubes (1¼ cups)
 ⅓ cup drained bottled roasted red bell peppers, cut into thin strips
 1 tablespoon butter
 ½ cup (2 ounces) shredded sharp Cheddar cheese

1. Preheat broiler.

2. Beat eggs, egg whites, salt and black pepper in large bowl until blended. Stir in broccoli, ham and pepper strips.

3. Melt butter over medium heat in 10-inch ovenproof skillet with sloping side. Pour egg mixture into skillet; cover. Cook 5 to 6 minutes or until eggs are set around edge. (Center will be wet.)

4. Uncover; sprinkle cheese over frittata. Transfer skillet to broiler; broil, 5 inches from heat, 2 minutes or until eggs are set in center and cheese is melted. Let stand 5 minutes; cut into wedges.

nutrients per serving: 211 Calories, 5g Carbohydrate, 1g Dietary Fiber, 13g Total Fat, 6g Saturated Fat, 201mg Cholesterol, 995mg Sodium, 19g Protein

Ham & Cheddar Frittata

Spinach & Egg Casserole

Makes 4 servings

1 box (10 ounces) BIRDS EYE® frozen Chopped Spinach
1 can (15 ounces) Cheddar cheese soup
1 tablespoon mustard
½ pound deli ham, cut into ¼-inch cubes
4 hard-boiled eggs, chopped or sliced

• Preheat oven to 350°F.

• In large saucepan, cook spinach according to package directions; drain well.

• Stir in soup, mustard and ham.

• Pour into 9×9-inch baking pan. Top with eggs.

• Bake 15 to 20 minutes or until heated through.

Prep Time: 10 minutes
Cook Time: 15 to 20 minutes

Serving Suggestion: Sprinkle with paprika for added color.

Birds Eye Idea: Cook the eggs the day before and refrigerate. They will be much easier to peel.

nutrients per serving: 234 Calories, 4g Carbohydrate, 2g Dietary Fiber, 14g Total Fat, 5g Saturated Fat, 249mg Cholesterol, 761mg Sodium, 21g Protein

Spinach & Egg Casserole

Feta Brunch Bake

Makes 4 servings

1 medium red bell pepper
2 bags (10 ounces each) fresh spinach, washed and stemmed
6 eggs
6 ounces crumbled feta cheese
⅓ cup chopped onion
2 tablespoons chopped fresh parsley
¼ teaspoon dried dill weed
 Dash black pepper

Preheat broiler. Place bell pepper on foil-lined broiler pan. Broil, 4 inches from heat, 15 to 20 minutes or until blackened on all sides, turning every 5 minutes with tongs. Place in paper bag; close bag and set aside to cool about 15 to 20 minutes. To peel pepper, cut around core, twist and remove. Cut in half and peel off skin with paring knife; rinse under cold water to remove seeds. Cut into ½-inch pieces.

To blanch spinach, place 1 quart water in 2-quart saucepan over high heat; bring to a boil. Add spinach. Return to a boil; boil 2 to 3 minutes or until crisp-tender. Drain; immediately plunge into cold water. Drain; let stand until cool enough to handle. Squeeze spinach to remove excess water; finely chop.

Preheat oven to 400°F. Grease 1-quart baking dish. Beat eggs in large bowl with electric mixer at medium speed until foamy. Stir in bell pepper, spinach, cheese, onion, parsley, dill weed and black pepper. Pour egg mixture into prepared dish. Bake 20 minutes or until set. Let stand 5 minutes before serving. Garnish as desired.

nutrients per serving: 266 Calories, 10g Carbohydrate, 4g Dietary Fiber, 17g Total Fat, 9g Saturated Fat, 359mg Cholesterol, 684mg Sodium, 20g Protein

Feta Brunch Bake

Triple-Decker Vegetable Omelet
Makes 4 servings

1 cup finely chopped broccoli
½ cup *each* diced red bell pepper and shredded carrot
⅓ cup sliced green onions
1 clove garlic, minced
2½ teaspoons FLEISCHMANN'S® Original Margarine, divided
¾ cup low fat cottage cheese (1% milkfat), divided
1 tablespoon plain dry bread crumbs
1 tablespoon grated Parmesan cheese
½ teaspoon Italian seasoning
1½ cups EGG BEATERS®, divided
⅓ cup chopped tomato
   Chopped fresh parsley, for garnish

In 8-inch nonstick skillet, over medium-high heat, sauté broccoli, bell pepper, carrot, green onions and garlic in 1 teaspoon margarine until tender. Remove from skillet; stir in ½ cup cottage cheese. Keep warm. Combine bread crumbs, Parmesan cheese and Italian seasoning; set aside.

In same skillet, over medium heat, melt ½ teaspoon margarine. Pour ½ cup Egg Beaters® into skillet. Cook, lifting edges to allow uncooked portion to flow underneath. When almost set, slide unfolded omelet onto ovenproof serving platter. Top with half each of the vegetable mixture and bread crumb mixture; set aside.

Prepare 2 more omelets with remaining Egg Beaters® and margarine. Layer 1 omelet onto serving platter over vegetable and bread crumb mixture; top with remaining vegetable mixture and bread crumb mixture. Layer with remaining omelet. Top omelet with remaining cottage cheese and tomato. Bake at 425°F for 5 to 7 minutes or until heated through. Garnish with parsley. Cut into wedges to serve.

nutrients per serving (1 wedge (¼ of total recipe) without garnish): 130 Calories, 9g Carbohydrate, 2g Dietary Fiber, 3g Total Fat, 1g Saturated Fat, 3mg Cholesterol, 411mg Sodium, 16g Protein

Triple-Decker Vegetable Omelet

Cheddary Sausage Frittata

Makes 4 servings

4 eggs
¼ cup milk
1 package (12 ounces) bulk pork breakfast sausage
1 poblano pepper,* seeded and chopped
1 cup (4 ounces) shredded Cheddar cheese

Poblano peppers can sting and irritate the skin; wear rubber gloves when handling peppers and do not touch eyes. Wash hands after handling.

1. Preheat broiler.

2. Combine eggs and milk in medium bowl; whisk until well blended. Set aside.

3. Heat 12-inch ovenproof nonstick skillet over medium-high heat until hot. Add sausage; cook and stir 4 minutes or until no longer pink, breaking up sausage with spoon. Drain sausage on paper towels; set aside.

4. Add pepper to same skillet; cook and stir 2 minutes or until crisp-tender. Return sausage to skillet with egg mixture; stir until blended. Cover; cook over medium-low heat 10 minutes or until eggs are almost set.

5. Sprinkle cheese over frittata; broil 2 minutes or until cheese is melted. Cut into 4 wedges. Serve immediately.

Tip: If skillet is not ovenproof, wrap handle in heavy-duty aluminum foil.

nutrients per serving: 423 Calories, 4g Carbohydrate, <1g Dietary Fiber, 31g Total Fat, 14g Saturated Fat, 298mg Cholesterol, 660mg Sodium, 27g Protein

Cheddary Sausage Frittata

Scrambled Eggs with Tomatoes & Chilies

Makes 4 servings

8 eggs
½ teaspoon salt
2 tablespoons butter or margarine
2 tablespoons vegetable oil
⅓ cup finely chopped onion
2 to 4 fresh serrano chilies,* finely chopped
2 medium tomatoes, seeded, chopped and drained
    Warm corn tortillas (optional)
    Fresh fruit (optional)

Serrano chilies can sting and irritate the skin; wear rubber gloves when handling peppers and do not touch eyes. Wash hands after handling.

1. Whisk eggs and salt lightly in medium bowl; set aside.

2. Heat butter and oil in large skillet over medium heat until hot. Add onion and chilies. Cook and stir 45 seconds or until hot but not soft.

3. Stir in tomatoes. Increase heat to medium-high. Cook and stir 45 seconds or until tomatoes are hot.

4. Add egg mixture all at once to skillet. Cook without stirring 1 minute. Cook 2 to 3 minutes more, stirring lightly until eggs are softly set. Serve with tortillas and fruit, if desired.

Note: Fresh chilies provide crunchy texture that cannot be duplicated with canned chilies. For milder flavor, remove the seeds from some or all of the chilies.

nutrients per serving: 282 Calories, 5g Carbohydrate, 1g Dietary Fiber, 23g Total Fat, 8g Saturated Fat, 441mg Cholesterol, 485mg Sodium, 13g Protein

Scrambled Eggs with Tomatoes & Chilies

Garden Omelet

Makes 2 servings

3 teaspoons butter or margarine, divided
⅓ cup chopped onion
⅓ cup chopped red bell pepper
½ cup sliced mushrooms
½ teaspoon dried basil leaves
4 eggs, beaten
1 tablespoon milk
¼ teaspoon black pepper
   Dash salt
½ cup (2 ounces) shredded Swiss cheese

1. Melt 1 teaspoon butter in large nonstick skillet over medium heat. Cook and stir onion and bell pepper 2 to 3 minutes or until onion is tender. Add mushrooms and basil; cook and stir 3 to 5 minutes. Remove from skillet; keep warm.

2. Whisk together eggs, milk, black pepper and salt in medium bowl. Melt remaining 2 teaspoons butter in same skillet over medium heat; rotate pan to coat bottom. Pour egg mixture into skillet. Cook over medium heat; as eggs begin to set, gently lift edges of omelet with spatula and tilt skillet so that uncooked portion flows underneath.

3. When eggs are fully cooked, spoon vegetable mixture over half of omelet. Sprinkle with cheese. Loosen omelet with spatula and fold in half. Transfer to warm serving plate.

Prep and Cook Time: 20 minutes

nutrients per serving (½ of omelet): 340 Calories, 9g Carbohydrate, 1g Dietary Fiber, 24g Total Fat, 17g Saturated Fat, 468mg Cholesterol, 264mg Sodium, 22g Protein

Garden Omelet

Vegetable Strata

Makes 6 servings

2 slices white bread, cubed
¼ cup shredded reduced-fat Swiss cheese
½ cup sliced carrots
½ cup sliced mushrooms
¼ cup chopped onion
1 clove garlic, crushed
1 teaspoon FLEISCHMANN'S® Original Margarine
½ cup chopped tomato
½ cup snow peas
1 cup EGG BEATERS®
¾ cup skim milk

Place bread cubes evenly on bottom of greased 1½-quart casserole dish. Sprinkle with cheese; set aside.

In medium nonstick skillet, over medium heat, sauté carrots, mushrooms, onion and garlic in margarine until tender. Stir in tomato and snow peas; cook 1 to 2 minutes more. Spoon over cheese and bread cubes. In small bowl, combine Egg Beaters® and milk; pour over vegetable mixture. Bake at 375°F for 45 to 50 minutes or until knife inserted into center comes out clean. Let stand 10 minutes before serving.

Prep Time: 15 minutes
Cook Time: 55 minutes

nutrients per serving (⅙ of total recipe):
83 Calories, 10g Carbohydrate, 1g Dietary Fiber, 1g Total Fat,
<1g Saturated Fat, 3mg Cholesterol, 161mg Sodium, 8g Protein

Vegetable Strata

Enticing
appetizers

Smoked Salmon Roses
Makes 32 servings

  1 package (8 ounces) cream cheese, softened
  1 tablespoon prepared horseradish
  1 tablespoon minced fresh dill plus whole sprigs for garnish
  1 tablespoon half-and-half
16 slices (12 to 16 ounces) smoked salmon
  1 red bell pepper, cut into thin strips

1. Combine cream cheese, horseradish, minced dill and half-and-half in small bowl. Beat until light and creamy.

2. Spread 1 tablespoon cream cheese mixture over each salmon slice. Roll up jelly-roll fashion. Slice each roll in half crosswise. Stand salmon rolls, cut side up, on serving dish to resemble roses. Garnish each "rose" by tucking 1 pepper strip and 1 dill sprig in center.

nutrients per serving (1 "rose"): 40 Calories, 1g Carbohydrate, <1g Dietary Fiber, 3g Total Fat, 2g Saturated Fat, 10mg Cholesterol, 106mg Sodium, 3g Protein

Smoked Salmon Roses

Peppered Shrimp Skewers

Makes 16 servings

16 (12-inch) wooden skewers
⅓ cup teriyaki sauce
⅓ cup ketchup
2 tablespoons dry sherry or water
2 tablespoons reduced-fat peanut butter
1 teaspoon hot pepper sauce
¼ teaspoon ground ginger
32 raw large shrimp (about 1½ pounds)
2 large yellow bell peppers
32 fresh sugar snap peas, trimmed

1. To prevent burning, soak skewers in water at least 20 minutes before assembling kabobs.

2. Coat rack of broiler pan with nonstick cooking spray; set aside.

3. Combine teriyaki sauce, ketchup, sherry, peanut butter, pepper sauce and ginger in small saucepan. Bring to a boil, stirring constantly. Reduce heat to low; simmer, uncovered, 1 minute. Remove from heat; set aside.

4. Peel and devein shrimp, leaving tails intact.

5. Cut each bell pepper lengthwise into 4 quarters; remove stems and seeds. Cut each quarter crosswise into 4 equal pieces. Thread 2 shrimp, bell pepper pieces and sugar snap peas onto each skewer; place on prepared broiler pan. Brush with teriyaki sauce mixture.

6. Broil 4 inches from heat 3 minutes; turn over. Brush with teriyaki sauce mixture; broil 2 minutes longer or until shrimp turn pink. Discard any remaining teriyaki sauce mixture. Transfer skewers to serving plates. Garnish, if desired.

nutrients per serving (1 skewer): 69 Calories, 6g Carbohydrate, 1g Dietary Fiber, 1g Total Fat, <1g Saturated Fat, 66mg Cholesterol, 258mg Sodium, 8g Protein

Peppered Shrimp Skewer

Great Zukes Pizza Bites

Makes 8 servings

1 medium zucchini
3 tablespoons pizza sauce
2 tablespoons tomato paste
¼ teaspoon crushed dried oregano
¾ cup shredded reduced-fat mozzarella cheese
¼ cup shredded Parmesan cheese
8 slices ripe olives
8 slices pepperoni

1. Preheat broiler and set rack 4 inches from heat.

2. Wash zucchini and trim off ends. Slice ¼ inch thick on diagonal to make 16 slices. Place zucchini on wire rack over nonstick cookie sheet.

3. Combine pizza sauce, tomato paste and oregano in small bowl; stir until well blended. Spread scant teaspoon of sauce over each zucchini slice. Combine mozzarella and Parmesan cheeses in small bowl. Top each zucchini slice with 1 tablespoon cheese mixture, pressing down into sauce. Place 1 olive slice on each of 8 pizza bites. Fold each pepperoni slice; place one folded pepperoni slice on each of remaining 8 pizza bites.

4. Broil 3 minutes or until cheese melts and zucchini is tender. Serve immediately.

nutrients per serving (2 pizza bites): 75 Calories, 3g Carbohydrate, 1g Dietary Fiber, 5g Total Fat, 2g Saturated Fat, 10mg Cholesterol, 288mg Sodium, 5g Protein

Great Zukes Pizza Bites

Mini Marinated Beef Skewers

Makes 6 servings (3 skewers each)

1 beef top round steak (about 1 pound)
2 tablespoons reduced-sodium soy sauce
1 tablespoon dry sherry
1 teaspoon dark sesame oil
2 cloves garlic, minced
18 cherry tomatoes (optional)

1. Cut beef crosswise into ⅛-inch slices. Place in large resealable plastic food storage bag. Combine soy sauce, sherry, oil and garlic in cup; pour over beef. Seal bag; turn to coat. Marinate in refrigerator at least 30 minutes or up to 2 hours.

2. Soak 18 (6-inch) wooden skewers in water 20 minutes.

3. Preheat broiler. Drain beef; discard marinade. Weave beef accordion-style onto skewers. Place on rack of broiler pan.

4. Broil 4 to 5 inches from heat 2 minutes. Turn skewers over; broil 2 minutes or until beef is barely pink.

5. Garnish each skewer with 1 cherry tomato, if desired. Place skewers on lettuce-lined platter. Serve warm.

nutrients per serving (3 skewers without cherry tomatoes and lettuce): 120 Calories, 2g Carbohydrate, <1g Dietary Fiber, 4g Total Fat, 1g Saturated Fat, 60mg Cholesterol, 99mg Sodium, 20g Protein

Mini Marinated Beef Skewers

Pinwheel Appetizers

Makes 36 appetizers

  3 cups cooked wild rice
  1 package (8 ounces) nonfat pasteurized process cream cheese product
  ⅓ cup grated Parmesan cheese
  1 teaspoon dried parsley flakes
  ½ teaspoon garlic powder
  ½ teaspoon Dijon-style mustard
  2 to 3 drops hot pepper sauce (optional)
  3 (12-inch) soft flour tortillas
  2½ ounces thinly sliced corned beef
  9 fresh spinach leaves

Combine wild rice, cream cheese, Parmesan cheese, parsley, garlic powder, mustard and pepper sauce. Spread evenly over tortillas, leaving ½-inch border on one side of each tortilla. Place single layer corned beef over rice and cheese mixture. Top with layer of spinach. Roll each tortilla tightly toward ½-inch border. Moisten border of tortilla with water; press to seal roll. Wrap tightly in plastic wrap. Refrigerate several hours or overnight. Cut into 1-inch slices to serve.

Favorite recipe from **Minnesota Cultivated Wild Rice Council**

> *nutrients per serving (1 appetizer):* 37 Calories, 5g Carbohydrate, <1g Dietary Fiber, 1g Total Fat, <1g Saturated Fat, 4mg Cholesterol, 91mg Sodium, 2g Protein

Pinwheel Appetizers

Rosemary-Scented Nut Mix

Makes 32 servings

2 tablespoons unsalted butter
2 cups pecan halves
1 cup unsalted macadamia nuts
1 cup walnuts
1 teaspoon dried rosemary, crushed
½ teaspoon salt
¼ teaspoon red pepper flakes

1. Preheat oven to 300°F. Melt butter in large saucepan over low heat. Add pecans, macadamia nuts and walnuts; mix well. Add rosemary, salt and red pepper flakes; cook and stir about 1 minute.

2. Pour mixture onto ungreased nonstick baking sheet. Bake 15 minutes, stirring mixture occasionally.

nutrients per serving (2 tablespoons): **108** Calories, **2g** Carbohydrate, **1g** Dietary Fiber, **11g** Total Fat, **2g** Saturated Fat, **2mg** Cholesterol, **37mg** Sodium, **2g** Protein

Rosemary-Scented Nut Mix

Individual Spinach & Bacon Quiches
Makes 10 servings

3 strips bacon
½ small onion, diced
1 package (9 ounces) frozen chopped spinach, thawed, drained and
   squeezed dry
½ teaspoon black pepper
⅛ teaspoon ground nutmeg
   Pinch salt
1 container (15-ounces) whole milk ricotta cheese
2 cups (8 ounces) shredded mozzarella cheese
1 cup (4 ounces) grated Parmesan cheese
3 eggs, lightly beaten

1. Preheat oven to 350°F. Spray 10 muffin pan cups with
nonstick cooking spray.

2. Cook bacon in large skillet over medium-high heat until
crisp. Drain; let cool and crumble.

3. In same skillet, cook and stir onion in remaining bacon fat
5 minutes or until tender. Add spinach, pepper, nutmeg and salt.
Cook and stir over medium heat about 3 minutes or until liquid
evaporates. Remove from heat and stir in bacon; let cool.

4. Combine ricotta, mozzarella and Parmesan cheese in large
bowl. Add eggs; stir until well blended. Add cooled spinach
mixture; mix well.

5. Divide mixture evenly among prepared muffin cups. Bake
40 minutes or until filling is set. Let stand 10 minutes. Run thin
knife around edges to release. Serve hot or refrigerate and serve
cold.

nutrients per serving (1 quiche): **216** Calories,
4g Carbohydrate, 1g Dietary Fiber, 15g Total Fat, 9g Saturated
Fat, 105mg Cholesterol, 405mg Sodium, 17g Protein

Individual Spinach & Bacon Quiches

Chilled Shrimp in Chinese Mustard Sauce

Makes 6 servings

1 cup water
½ cup dry white wine
2 tablespoons reduced-sodium soy sauce
½ teaspoon Szechuan or black peppercorns
1 pound raw large shrimp, peeled and deveined
¼ cup prepared sweet and sour sauce
2 teaspoons hot Chinese mustard

1. Combine water, wine, soy sauce and peppercorns in medium saucepan. Bring to a boil over high heat. Add shrimp; reduce heat to medium. Cover and simmer 2 to 3 minutes or until shrimp are opaque and cooked through. Drain well. Cover and refrigerate until chilled.

2. For mustard sauce, combine sweet and sour sauce and mustard in small bowl; mix well. Serve with shrimp.

Note: For this quick and easy recipe, the shrimp can be prepared up to one day in advance. If you are unable to find hot Chinese mustard or simply want a sauce with less heat, substitute a spicy brown or Dijon-style mustard.

nutrients per serving (⅙ of total recipe with about 2 teaspoons mustard sauce): 92 Calories, 5g Carbohydrate, <1g Dietary Fiber, 1g Total Fat, <1g Saturated Fat, 116mg Cholesterol, 365mg Sodium, 13g Protein

Chilled Shrimp in Chinese Mustard Sauce

Parmesan-Pepper Crisps

Makes about 26 crisps

2 cups (4 ounces) loosely packed coarsely-grated Parmesan cheese
2 teaspoons freshly ground black pepper

1. Preheat oven to 450°F. Line wire racks with paper towels.

2. Place heaping teaspoonfuls cheese 2 inches apart on ungreased nonstick baking sheet. Flatten cheese mounds with back of spoon. Sprinkle each mound with pinch of pepper.

3. Bake 15 to 20 minutes or until crisps are very lightly browned. (Watch closely—crisps burn easily.) Let cool on baking sheet 2 minutes; carefully remove with spatula to prepared racks. Store in airtight container in refrigerator up to 3 days.

nutrients per serving (1 crisp): 28 Calories, <1g Carbohydrate, <1g Dietary Fiber, 2g Total Fat, 1g Saturated Fat, 5mg Cholesterol, 115mg Sodium, 3g Protein

Hot Artichoke Dip

Makes 40 (1 tablespoon) servings

1 can (14 ounces) artichoke hearts, drained and chopped
1 cup CARB OPTIONS™ Whipped Dressing
1 cup grated Parmesan cheese (about 4 ounces)
1 clove garlic, finely chopped or ¼ teaspoon LAWRY'S® Garlic Powder With Parsley (optional)

1. Preheat oven to 350°F.

2. In 1-quart casserole, combine all ingredients. Bake uncovered 25 minutes or until heated through. Serve with your favorite dippers.

nutrients per serving (1 tablespoon dip without dippers): 35 Calories, 1g Carbohydrate, 0g Dietary Fiber, 3g Total Fat, 1g Saturated Fat, 5mg Cholesterol, 110mg Sodium, 1g Protein

Parmesan-Pepper Crisps

Mushrooms Rockefeller

Makes 18 appetizers

18 large fresh button mushrooms (about 1 pound)
2 slices bacon
¼ cup chopped onion
1 package (10 ounces) frozen chopped spinach, thawed and
    squeezed dry
1 tablespoon lemon juice
1 teaspoon grated lemon peel
½ jar (2 ounces) chopped pimiento, drained
    Lemon slices and lemon balm for garnish (optional)

1. Lightly spray 13×9-inch baking dish with nonstick cooking
spray. Preheat oven to 375°F. Brush dirt from mushrooms; clean
by wiping mushrooms with damp paper towel. Pull entire stem
out of each mushroom cap.

2. Cut thin slice from base of each stem; discard. Chop stems.

3. Cook bacon in medium skillet over medium heat until
crisp. Remove bacon with tongs to paper towel; set aside. Add
mushroom stems and onion to hot drippings in skillet. Cook and
stir until onion is soft. Add spinach, lemon juice, lemon peel and
pimiento; blend well.

4. Stuff mushroom caps with spinach mixture; place in single
layer in prepared baking dish. Crumble bacon; sprinkle over
tops of mushrooms. Bake 15 minutes or until heated through.
Garnish, if desired. Serve immediately.

nutrients per serving (1 stuffed mushroom cap):
17 Calories, 2g Carbohydrate, 1g Dietary Fiber, 1g Total Fat,
<1g Saturated Fat, 1mg Cholesterol, 26mg Sodium, 2g Protein

Mushrooms Rockefeller

Ham and Cheese "Sushi" Rolls

Makes 8 servings

4 thin slices deli ham (about 4×4 inches)
1 package (8 ounces) cream cheese, softened
1 piece (4 inches long) seedless cucumber, quartered lengthwise
    (about ½ cucumber)
4 thin slices (about 4×4 inches) American or Cheddar cheese, at
    room temperature
1 red bell pepper, cut into thin 4-inch-long strips

1. For ham sushi, pat 1 ham slice with paper towel to remove
excess moisture. Spread 2 tablespoons cream cheese to edges of
ham slice. Pat 1 cucumber piece with paper towel to remove
excess moisture; place at edge of ham slice. Roll up tightly,
pressing gently to seal. Wrap in plastic wrap; refrigerate. Repeat
with remaining ham slices, cream cheese and cucumber pieces.

2. For cheese sushi, spread 2 tablespoons cream cheese to edges
of 1 cheese slice. Place 2 strips red pepper at edge of cheese slice.
Roll up tightly, pressing gently to seal. Wrap in plastic wrap;
refrigerate. Repeat with remaining cheese slices, cream cheese
and red pepper strips.

3. To serve, remove plastic wrap from ham and cheese rolls. Cut
each roll into 8 (½-inch-wide) pieces.

> *nutrients per serving (8 pieces):* 145 Calories,
> 3g Carbohydrate, <1g Dietary Fiber, 13g Total Fat, 12g Saturated
> Fat, 40mg Cholesterol, 263mg Sodium, 5g Protein

Ham and Cheese "Sushi" Rolls

Spicy Orange Chicken Kabob Appetizers

Makes 12 servings

　2 boneless skinless chicken breasts (about 8 ounces)
　1 small red or green bell pepper
　24 small fresh button mushrooms
　½ cup orange juice
　2 tablespoons reduced-sodium soy sauce
　1 tablespoon vegetable oil
1½ teaspoons onion powder
　½ teaspoon Chinese five-spice powder*

Chinese five-spice powder is a blend of cinnamon, cloves, fennel seed, anise and Szechuan peppercorns. It is available in most supermarkets and at Asian grocery stores.

1. Cut chicken and bell pepper into 24 (¾-inch) square pieces. Place chicken, pepper and mushrooms in large resealable plastic food storage bag. Combine orange juice, soy sauce, oil, onion powder and five-spice powder in small bowl. Pour over chicken mixture. Seal bag securely; turn to coat. Marinate in refrigerator 4 to 24 hours, turning frequently.

2. Soak 24 small wooden skewers or toothpicks in water 20 minutes. Meanwhile, preheat broiler. Coat broiler pan with nonstick cooking spray.

3. Drain chicken mixture, reserving marinade. Thread 1 piece chicken, 1 piece pepper and 1 mushroom onto each skewer. Place on prepared pan. Brush with marinade; discard remaining marinade. Broil 4 inches from heat 5 to 6 minutes or until chicken is no longer pink in center. Serve immediately.

nutrients per serving (2 kabobs): **30 Calories, 2g Carbohydrate, <1g Dietary Fiber, <1g Total Fat, <1g Saturated Fat, 10mg Cholesterol, 38mg Sodium, 4g Protein**

Spicy Orange Chicken Kabob Appetizers

Easiest Three-Cheese Fondue

Makes 8 (3-tablespoon) servings

1 tablespoon margarine
¼ cup finely chopped onion
2 cloves garlic, minced
1 tablespoon all-purpose flour
¾ cup reduced-fat (2%) milk
2 cups (8 ounces) shredded mild or sharp Cheddar cheese
1 package (3 ounces) cream cheese, cut into cubes
½ cup (2 ounces) crumbled blue cheese
⅛ teaspoon ground red pepper
4 to 6 drops hot pepper sauce
    Assorted fresh vegetables for dipping

1. Heat margarine in small saucepan over medium heat until melted. Add onion and garlic; cook and stir 2 to 3 minutes or until tender. Stir in flour; cook 2 minutes, stirring constantly.

2. Stir milk into saucepan; bring to a boil. Boil, stirring constantly, about 1 minute or until thickened. Reduce heat to low; add cheeses, stirring until melted. Stir in red pepper and pepper sauce. Pour fondue into serving dish. Serve with dippers.

Prep and Cook Time: 20 minutes

Lighten Up: To reduce the total fat, replace the Cheddar cheese and cream cheese with reduced-fat Cheddar and cream cheeses.

nutrients per serving (3 tablespoons fondue without dippers): 207 Calories, 3g Carbohydrate, <1g Dietary Fiber, 17g Total Fat, 10g Saturated Fat, 48mg Cholesterol, 334mg Sodium, 10g Protein

Easiest Three-Cheese Fondue

Curly Lettuce Wrappers

Makes 4 servings

4 green leaf lettuce leaves
¼ cup reduced-fat sour cream
4 turkey bacon slices, crisp-cooked and crumbled
½ cup (2 ounces) crumbled feta or blue cheese
8 ounces thinly sliced deli turkey breast
4 whole green onions
½ medium red or green bell pepper, thinly sliced
1 cup broccoli sprouts

1. Rinse lettuce leaves and pat dry.

2. Combine sour cream and bacon in small bowl. Spread ¼ of sour cream mixture evenly over center third of one lettuce leaf. Sprinkle 2 tablespoons cheese over sour cream. Top with 2 ounces turkey.

3. Cut off green portion of each green onion, reserving white onion bottoms for another use. Place green portion of 1 onion, ¼ of bell pepper slices and ¼ cup sprouts on top of turkey.

4. Fold right edge of lettuce over filling; fold bottom edge up over filling. Loosely roll up from folded right edge, leaving left edge of wrap open. Repeat with remaining ingredients.

nutrients per serving (1 lettuce wrapper):
155 Calories, 6g Carbohydrate, <1g Dietary Fiber, 7g Total Fat, 4g Saturated Fat, 75mg Cholesterol, 987mg Sodium, 17g Protein

Curly Lettuce Wrapper

Skewered Chicken Satay

Makes 4 main-dish or 12 appetizer servings

1 cup CARB OPTIONS™ Italian Dressing
4 teaspoons soy sauce
½ teaspoon ground ginger
1 pound boneless, skinless chicken breast halves, cut into thin strips
¼ cup CARB OPTIONS™ Creamy Peanut Spread
1 tablespoon finely chopped green onion
¼ teaspoon crushed red pepper flakes (optional)
½ teaspoon SPLENDA® No Calorie Sweetener

1. For marinade, in medium bowl, whisk together Carb Options Italian Dressing, soy sauce and ginger. In large, shallow nonaluminum baking dish or plastic bag, pour ¼ cup marinade over chicken and turn to coat. Cover, or close bag, and marinate in refrigerator, turning occasionally, up to 3 hours. Refrigerate ¼ cup remaining marinade.

2. Meanwhile, in small bowl, whisk together remaining ½ cup marinade, Carb Options Creamy Peanut Spread, green onion, red pepper flakes and Splenda®; set aside for dipping sauce. Soak 12 (6-inch) wooden skewers in water for at least 30 minutes.

3. Remove chicken from marinade, discarding marinade. Thread chicken on skewers. Grill or broil chicken, turning once and brushing frequently with ¼ cup reserved marinade, until chicken is thoroughly cooked. Serve with peanut dipping sauce.

Preparation Time: 10 minutes
Marinate Time: 3 hours
Cook Time: 5 minutes

nutrients per serving (3 skewers): 330 Calories, 4g Carbohydrate, 1g Dietary Fiber, 23g Total Fat, 5g Saturated Fat, 65mg Cholesterol, 910mg Sodium, 28g Protein

Eggplant Caviar

Makes 1½ cups

1 large eggplant, unpeeled
¼ cup chopped onion
2 tablespoons lemon juice
1 tablespoon olive or vegetable oil
1 small clove garlic
½ teaspoon salt
½ teaspoon TABASCO® brand Pepper Sauce
   Sieved hard-cooked egg white (optional)
   Lemon slices (optional)

Preheat oven to 350°F. Place eggplant in shallow baking dish. Bake 1 hour or until soft, turning once. Trim off ends; slice eggplant in half lengthwise. Place cut-side-down in colander and let drain 10 minutes. Scoop out pulp; reserve pulp and peel. Combine eggplant peel, onion, lemon juice, oil, garlic, salt and TABASCO® Sauce in blender or food processor. Cover and process until peel is finely chopped. Add eggplant pulp. Cover and process just until chopped. Place in serving dish. Garnish with egg white and lemon slices, if desired. Serve with toast points.

nutrients per serving (1 tablespoon Eggplant Caviar (without toast points and garnish)):
14 Calories, 2g Carbohydrate, 1g Dietary Fiber, 1g Total Fat, <1g Saturated Fat, 0mg Cholesterol, 50mg Sodium, <1g Protein

u n b e a t a b l e
sides

Stir-Fried Asparagus
Makes 6 servings

½ pound asparagus
1 tablespoon olive or canola oil
1 cup sliced celery
½ cup bottled roasted red peppers, drained and diced
¼ teaspoon black pepper
¼ cup sliced almonds, toasted*

*To toast almonds, place in small dry skillet. Cook over medium heat, stirring constantly, until almonds are lightly browned.

1. Trim ends from asparagus; cut stalks diagonally into 1-inch pieces.

2. Heat oil in 12-inch nonstick skillet over medium-high heat. Add celery; stir-fry 2 minutes. Add asparagus and red peppers; stir-fry 3 to 4 minutes or until asparagus is crisp-tender.

3. Add black pepper and almonds; stir until blended.

nutrients per serving: 67 Calories, 4g Carbohydrate, 2g Dietary Fiber, 5g Total Fat, <1g Saturated Fat, 0mg Cholesterol, 18mg Sodium, 2g Protein

Stir-Fried Asparagus

Roasted Fall Vegetables

Makes 6 servings

2 cups small broccoli florets
1 large red bell pepper, cut into 1-inch squares
1 cup cubed turnip (1-inch cubes)
½ cup diced onion
1 tablespoon balsamic vinegar or red wine vinegar
2 teaspoons olive oil
½ cup fat-free reduced-sodium chicken broth or water
4 sprigs fresh thyme *or* ¼ teaspoon dried thyme leaves
¼ teaspoon salt
Black pepper to taste

1. Preheat oven to 425°F. Combine broccoli, bell pepper, turnip and onion in shallow heavy roasting pan.

2. Whisk together vinegar and oil; pour over vegetables, tossing to coat. Pour chicken broth around vegetables. Add thyme sprigs.

3. Roast vegetables about 30 minutes or until tender, stirring occasionally. Remove from oven; sprinkle with salt and black pepper.

nutrients per serving (⅓ cup vegetables):
36 Calories, 4g Carbohydrate, 2g Dietary Fiber, 2g Total Fat,
<1g Saturated Fat, 0mg Cholesterol, 133mg Sodium, 2g Protein

Roasted Fall Vegetables

Broiled Zucchini Halves

Makes 4 side-dish servings

½ cup (2 ounces) shredded mozzarella cheese
2 tablespoons diced pimiento
2 tablespoons chopped ripe olives
4 small zucchini (about 1 pound total), sliced lengthwise
1 tablespoon olive oil

1. Preheat broiler; place oven rack 6 inches below heat source. Combine cheese, pimiento and olives in small bowl; set aside.

2. Brush both sides of zucchini halves with oil; arrange on broiler pan lined with foil. Broil 5 minutes or until fork-tender.

3. Spoon about 2 tablespoons cheese mixture along each zucchini half. Broil until cheese melts and browns. Serve immediately.

nutrients per serving: 94 Calories, 5g Carbohydrate, 1g Dietary Fiber, 7g Total Fat, 2g Saturated Fat, 8mg Cholesterol, 144mg Sodium, 5g Protein

Asian Green Beans

Makes 6 servings

1 tablespoon BERTOLLI® Classico Olive Oil
2 cloves garlic, finely chopped
1 pound green beans, trimmed
¼ cup CARB OPTIONS™ Asian Teriyaki Marinade
½ cup sliced almonds

1. In 12-inch skillet, heat olive oil over medium-high heat and cook garlic 30 seconds. Add green beans and Carb Options Asian Teriyaki Marinade and cook until beans are tender, 7 minutes. To serve, toss with almonds.

nutrients per serving: 130 Calories, 10g Carbohydrate, 4g Dietary Fiber, 9g Total Fat, 1g Saturated Fat, 0mg Cholesterol, 340mg Sodium, 4g Protein

Broiled Zucchini Halves

Light Lemon Cauliflower

Makes 6 servings

¼ cup chopped fresh parsley, divided
½ teaspoon grated lemon peel
6 cups (about 1½ pounds) cauliflower florets
1 tablespoon reduced-fat margarine
3 cloves garlic, minced
2 tablespoons fresh lemon juice
¼ cup shredded Parmesan cheese

1. Place 1 tablespoon parsley, lemon peel and about 1 inch of water in large saucepan. Place cauliflower in steamer basket and place in saucepan. Bring water to a boil over medium heat. Cover and steam 14 to 16 minutes or until cauliflower is crisp-tender. Remove to large bowl; keep warm. Reserve ½ cup hot liquid.

2. Heat margarine in small saucepan over medium heat. Add garlic; cook and stir 2 to 3 minutes or until soft. Stir in lemon juice and reserved liquid.

3. Spoon lemon sauce over cauliflower. Sprinkle with remaining 3 tablespoons parsley and cheese before serving. Garnish with lemon slices, if desired.

nutrients per serving (about ⅔ cup cauliflower with 1½ tablespoons sauce and 2 teaspoons cheese): 53 Calories, 6g Carbohydrate, 3g Dietary Fiber, 2g Total Fat, 1g Saturated Fat, 3mg Cholesterol, 116mg Sodium, 4g Protein

Light Lemon Cauliflower

Braised Oriental Cabbage

Makes 6 side-dish servings

½ small head green cabbage (about ½ pound)
1 small head bok choy (about ¾ pound)
½ cup fat-free reduced-sodium chicken broth
2 tablespoons rice wine vinegar
2 tablespoons reduced-sodium soy sauce
1 tablespoon brown sugar
¼ teaspoon red pepper flakes (optional)
1 tablespoon water
1 tablespoon cornstarch

1. Cut cabbage into 1-inch pieces. Trim and discard bottoms from bok choy; slice stems into ½-inch pieces. Cut tops of leaves into ½-inch slices; set aside.

2. Combine cabbage and bok choy stems in large nonstick skillet. Add broth, vinegar, soy sauce, brown sugar and red pepper flakes, if desired.

3. Bring to a boil over high heat. Reduce heat to medium. Cover and simmer 5 minutes or until vegetables are crisp-tender.

4. Blend water into cornstarch in small bowl until smooth. Stir into skillet. Cook and stir 1 minute or until sauce boils and thickens.

5. Stir in reserved bok choy leaves; cook 1 minute.

nutrients per serving: 34 Calories, 6g Carbohydrate, 1g Dietary Fiber, <1g Total Fat, <1g Saturated Fat, 0mg Cholesterol, 170mg Sodium, 2g Protein

Braised Oriental Cabbage

Asparagus with Sesame-Ginger Sauce

Makes 7 servings

1 tablespoon SPLENDA® No Calorie Sweetener, Granular
1 tablespoon water
1 tablespoon peanut oil
1 tablespoon rice vinegar
1 tablespoon soy sauce
1 tablespoon tahini* (puréed sesame seeds)
1 teaspoon chopped fresh ginger
½ teaspoon chopped garlic
  Pinch crushed red pepper
48 medium asparagus spears, trimmed and peeled

Look for tahini in the ethnic foods section of your supermarket.

1. In a food processor, combine all ingredients except asparagus and mix until thoroughly blended. Set aside.

2. Fill large skillet half-full of water; cover and bring to a boil. Add asparagus and simmer just until crisp-tender, approximately 4 to 5 minutes. Drain well. (Do not rinse.)

3. Transfer to serving platter. Pour sauce over hot asparagus. Serve warm or at room temperature.

Preparation Time: 10 minutes
Cooking Time: 5 minutes

> *nutrients per serving (⅔ cup or 4.3 ounces (121 g)):* 59 Calories, 6g Carbohydrate, 2g Dietary Fiber, 3g Total Fat, 1g Saturated Fat, 0mg Cholesterol, 183mg Sodium, 3g Protein

Asparagus with Sesame-Ginger Sauce

Marinated Vegetables

Makes 12 servings

¼ cup rice wine vinegar
3 tablespoons reduced-sodium soy sauce
2 tablespoons fresh lemon juice
1 tablespoon vegetable oil
1 clove garlic, minced
1 teaspoon minced fresh ginger
½ teaspoon sugar
2 cups broccoli florets
2 cups cauliflower florets
2 cups diagonally sliced carrots (½-inch pieces)
8 ounces whole fresh mushrooms
1 large red bell pepper, cut into 1-inch pieces
  Lettuce leaves

1. Combine vinegar, soy sauce, lemon juice, oil, garlic, ginger and sugar in large bowl. Set aside.

2. To blanch broccoli, cauliflower and carrots, cook 1 minute in enough salted boiling water to cover. Remove and plunge into cold water, then drain immediately. Add to oil mixture in bowl while still warm; toss to coat. Cool to room temperature.

3. Add mushrooms and bell pepper to vegetables in bowl; toss to coat. Cover and marinate in refrigerator at least 4 hours or up to 24 hours. Drain vegetables, reserving marinade.

4. Arrange vegetables on lettuce-lined platter. Serve chilled or at room temperature with toothpicks. Serve remaining marinade in small cup for dipping, if desired.

nutrients per serving (about ¾ cup vegetables with 1⅓ teaspoons marinade): **37 Calories, 6g Carbohydrate, 2g Dietary Fiber, 1g Total Fat, <1g Saturated Fat, 0mg Cholesterol, 146mg Sodium, 2g Protein**

Marinated Vegetables

Frenched Beans with Celery

Makes 6 side-dish servings

¾ pound fresh green beans
2 ribs celery
2 tablespoons butter, melted
2 tablespoons toasted sunflower seeds*
  Celery leaves and carrot slices for garnish

To toast sunflower seeds, heat ½ teaspoon oil in small skillet over medium heat. Add shelled sunflower seeds; cook and stir 3 minutes or until lightly browned, shaking pan constantly. Remove to paper towels.

1. Place beans in colander; rinse well. To prepare beans, snap off stem end from each bean, pulling strings down to remove if present. (Young tender beans may have no strings.)

2. Slice beans lengthwise; set aside.

3. To prepare celery, trim stem ends and leaves from ribs. Reserve leaves for garnish, if desired. Cut celery diagonally into thin slices.

4. Bring 1 inch of water in 2-quart saucepan to a boil over high heat. Add beans and celery. Cover; reduce heat to medium-low. Simmer 8 minutes or until beans are crisp-tender; drain.

5. Toss beans and celery with butter. Transfer to warm serving dish. Sprinkle with sunflower seeds. Garnish, if desired. Serve immediately.

nutrients per serving: 71 Calories, 5g Carbohydrate, 2g Dietary Fiber, 5g Total Fat, 2g Saturated Fat, 11mg Cholesterol, 43mg Sodium, 2g Protein

Frenched Beans with Celery

Roasted Red Pepper & Tomato Casserole

Makes 6 servings

1 jar (12 ounces) roasted red peppers, drained
1½ teaspoons red wine vinegar
1 teaspoon olive oil
1 clove garlic, minced
¼ teaspoon salt
¼ teaspoon black pepper
⅓ cup grated Parmesan cheese, divided
3 medium tomatoes (about 1½ pounds), sliced
½ cup (about 1 ounce) herb-flavored croutons, crushed

Microwave Directions

1. Combine red peppers, vinegar, oil, garlic, salt and black pepper in food processor; process, using on/off pulsing action, 1 minute or until slightly chunky. Reserve 2 tablespoons cheese. Stir remaining cheese into red pepper mixture.

2. Arrange tomato slices in 8-inch round microwavable baking dish; microwave at HIGH (100% power) 1 minute. Spoon red pepper mixture on top; microwave at HIGH 2 to 3 minutes or until tomatoes are slightly soft.

3. Sprinkle with reserved cheese and croutons. Garnish, if desired.

nutrients per serving: 80 Calories, 9g Carbohydrate, 1g Dietary Fiber, 2g Total Fat, 1g Saturated Fat, 3mg Cholesterol, 342mg Sodium, 3g Protein

Roasted Red Pepper & Tomato Casserole

Creamy Mashed Cauliflower

Makes 5 servings

2 cups water
1 medium head cauliflower, separated into florets (about 5 cups)
¼ cup CARB OPTIONS™ Whipped Dressing
¼ teaspoon salt

1. In 3-quart saucepot, bring water to a boil. Add cauliflower and cook covered 15 minutes or until florets are very tender; drain.

2. In food processor or blender, process cauliflower, Carb Options Whipped Dressing and salt until creamy, scraping sides as needed.

nutrients per serving (¼ of total recipe):
70 Calories, 6g Carbohydrate, 3g Dietary Fiber, 5g Total Fat,
0g Saturated Fat, 5mg Cholesterol, 230mg Sodium, 2g Protein

Hot and Spicy Cabbage Medley

Makes 8 servings

1 teaspoon CRISCO® Oil*
2 ounces smoked ham, chopped
½ cup *each* chopped green bell pepper and chopped onion
1 can (10 ounces) tomatoes with chilies, undrained and chopped
½ teaspoon sugar
4 cups sliced cabbage
⅛ teaspoon *each* black pepper and hot pepper sauce

Use your favorite Crisco Oil product.

1. Heat oil in large skillet on medium heat. Add ham, green pepper and onion. Cook and stir until vegetables are crisp-tender. Add tomatoes and sugar. Simmer 3 minutes.

2. Add remaining ingredients. Simmer 15 minutes, stirring often.

nutrients per serving (⅛ of total recipe):
32 Calories, 5g Carbohydrate, 2g Dietary Fiber, 1g Total Fat,
<1g Saturated Fat, 3mg Cholesterol, 179mg Sodium, 2g Protein

Savory Green Bean Casserole
Makes 8 servings

2 teaspoons CRISCO® Oil*
1 medium onion, chopped
½ medium green bell pepper, chopped
1 package (10 ounces) frozen green beans, thawed
1 can (8 ounces) tomatoes, drained
2 tablespoons nonfat mayonnaise dressing
¼ teaspoon salt
⅛ teaspoon crushed red pepper
⅛ teaspoon garlic powder
¼ cup plain dry bread crumbs

Use your favorite Crisco Oil product.

1. Heat oven to 375°F. Oil 1-quart casserole lightly. Place cooling rack on countertop.

2. Heat 2 teaspoons oil in large skillet on medium heat. Add onion and green pepper. Cook and stir until tender.

3. Add beans, tomatoes, mayonnaise dressing, salt, red pepper and garlic powder. Heat thoroughly, stirring occasionally.

4. Spoon into casserole. Sprinkle with bread crumbs. Bake at 375°F for 30 minutes. *Do not overbake.* Remove casserole to cooling rack. Serve warm.

nutrients per serving (½ cup casserole): **51 Calories, 8g Carbohydrate, 2g Dietary Fiber, 1g Total Fat, <1g Saturated Fat, 0mg Cholesterol, 179mg Sodium, 1g Protein**

Grilled Vegetables

Makes 6 servings

¼ cup minced fresh herbs, such as parsley, thyme, rosemary,
    oregano or basil
1 small eggplant (about ¾ pound), cut into ¼-inch-thick slices
½ teaspoon salt
1 *each* red, green and yellow bell pepper, quartered and seeded
2 zucchini, cut lengthwise into ¼-inch-thick slices
1 fennel bulb, cut lengthwise into ¼-inch-thick slices
    Nonstick cooking spray

1. Combine herbs in small bowl; let stand 3 hours or overnight.

2. Place eggplant in large colander over bowl; sprinkle with salt.
Drain 1 hour.

3. Heat grill until coals are glowing red. Spray vegetables
with cooking spray and sprinkle with herb mixture. Grill 10 to
15 minutes or until fork-tender and lightly browned on both sides.
(Cooking times vary depending on vegetable; remove vegetables as
they are done, to avoid overcooking.)

Variation: Cut vegetables into 1-inch cubes and thread onto
skewers. Spray with cooking spray and sprinkle with herb
mixture. Grill as directed above.

> *nutrients per serving:* 34 Calories, 8g Carbohydrate,
> 2g Dietary Fiber, <1g Total Fat, <1g Saturated Fat,
> 0mg Cholesterol, 190mg Sodium, 1g Protein

Grilled Vegetables

Citrus Asparagus

Makes 4 servings

Orange Sauce
    2 teaspoons reduced-fat margarine
    1 clove garlic, minced
    Juice of 1 large orange (about ⅓ cup)
1¼ teaspoons balsamic vinegar
    ¼ teaspoon Dijon mustard
    ½ teaspoon grated orange peel
    Salt (optional)

Asparagus
    Nonstick olive oil cooking spray
    1 small onion, diced
    1 pound fresh asparagus, lower halves of stalks peeled*
    ⅔ cup diced red bell pepper
    ½ cup water

*If using pencil-thin asparagus, do not peel. Reduce cooking time to 4 to 5 minutes.

1. For orange sauce, heat margarine in small saucepan over medium heat. Add garlic; cook and stir 2 minutes or until soft. Stir in orange juice; bring to a boil. Add vinegar and mustard; reduce heat and simmer 2 minutes. Remove from heat and add orange peel. Season to taste with salt, if desired; keep warm.

2. For asparagus, spray medium saucepan with cooking spray; heat over medium-high heat. Add onion; cook and stir 2 minutes. Add asparagus, bell pepper and water. Reduce heat to medium-low. Cover and simmer 7 minutes or until asparagus is crisp-tender. Remove vegetables with slotted spoon to serving dish; serve with orange sauce.

nutrients per serving: 58 Calories, 10g Carbohydrate, 2g Dietary Fiber, 1g Total Fat, <1g Saturated Fat, <1mg Cholesterol, 37mg Sodium, 3g Protein

Citrus Asparagus

Broccoli Boutonnieres and Buttons

Makes 6 servings

1 large bunch fresh broccoli (about 1½ pounds)
2 teaspoons lemon juice
1 tablespoon cornstarch
1 cup water
1 teaspoon instant chicken bouillon granules
  White pepper
  Lemon wedges and mizuna greens for garnish (optional)

1. Trim leaves from broccoli stalks. Cut broccoli into florets. Peel stems, then cut crosswise into ¼-inch pieces to make "buttons."

2. Place steamer basket in large saucepan; add 1 inch of water. (Water should not touch bottom of basket.) Place buttons in steamer; top with florets. Cover; bring to a boil over high heat. Steam 4 to 6 minutes or until bright green and crisp-tender, adding more water if necessary.

3. Meanwhile, combine lemon juice and cornstarch in small saucepan. Stir in water and bouillon. Cook over medium heat until mixture thickens and begins to boil, stirring constantly.

4. Arrange buttons around edge of warm serving plate. Place florets in center. Drizzle with sauce; season with pepper to taste. Garnish, if desired.

> *nutrients per serving:* 34 Calories, 6g Carbohydrate,
> 3g Dietary Fiber, <1g Total Fat, <1g Saturated Fat,
> 0mg Cholesterol, 198mg Sodium, 3g Protein

Broccoli Boutonnieres and Buttons

Hot and Spicy Spinach

Makes 4 servings

Nonstick cooking spray
1 red bell pepper, cut into 1-inch pieces
1 clove garlic, minced
1 pound fresh spinach, washed, stemmed and chopped
1 tablespoon prepared mustard
1 teaspoon lemon juice
¼ teaspoon red pepper flakes

1. Spray large skillet with cooking spray; heat over medium heat. Add bell pepper and garlic; cook and stir 3 minutes.

2. Add spinach; cook and stir 3 minutes or just until spinach begins to wilt.

3. Stir in remaining ingredients. Serve immediately.

nutrients per serving: 37 Calories, 6g Carbohydrate, 3g Dietary Fiber, 1g Total Fat, <1g Saturated Fat, 0mg Cholesterol, 138mg Sodium, 4g Protein

Marinated Beet Salad

Makes 8 servings

2 cans (15 ounces each) small, whole or sliced beets
½ cup white vinegar
¾ to 1 cup EQUAL® SPOONFUL*

May substitute 18 to 24 packets EQUAL® sweetener.

• Combine beets, beet juice, vinegar and Equal® in medium bowl; cover tightly.

• Chill at least 8 hours before serving. Drain before serving.

nutrients per serving (about ½ cup beets):
40 Calories, 10g Carbohydrate, 1g Dietary Fiber, 0g Total Fat, 0g Saturated Fat, 0mg Cholesterol, 22mg Sodium, 1g Protein

Hot and Spicy Spinach

Guiltless Zucchini

Makes 4 servings

    Nonstick cooking spray
 4 medium zucchini, sliced
 ⅓ cup chopped onion
 4 cloves garlic, minced
 ¼ teaspoon dried oregano leaves
 ½ cup GUILTLESS GOURMET® Roasted Red Pepper Salsa
 ¼ cup (1 ounce) shredded low-fat mozzarella cheese

Coat large nonstick skillet with cooking spray; heat over medium heat until hot. Add zucchini; cook and stir 5 minutes. Add onion, garlic and oregano; cook 5 minutes more or until zucchini and onion are lightly browned. Stir in salsa. Bring just to a boil. Reduce heat to low; simmer 5 minutes more or until zucchini is crisp-tender. Sprinkle cheese on top; cover and cook 1 to 2 minutes or until cheese melts. Serve hot.

nutrients per serving (¼ of total recipe):
58 Calories, 8g Carbohydrate, 2g Dietary Fiber, 1g Total Fat, <1g Saturated Fat, 4mg Cholesterol, 197mg Sodium, 4g Protein

Guiltless Zucchini

Indian-Style Vegetable Stir-Fry

Makes 6 servings

        1 teaspoon canola oil
        1 teaspoon curry powder
        1 teaspoon ground cumin
      ⅛ teaspoon red pepper flakes
    1½ teaspoons minced seeded jalapeño pepper*
        2 cloves garlic, minced
      ¾ cup chopped red bell pepper
      ¾ cup thinly sliced carrots
        3 cups cauliflower florets
      ½ cup water, divided
      ½ teaspoon salt
        2 teaspoons finely chopped fresh cilantro (optional)

Jalapeño peppers can sting and irritate the skin; wear rubber gloves when handling peppers and do not touch eyes. Wash hands after handling.

1. Heat oil in large nonstick skillet over medium-high heat. Add curry powder, cumin and red pepper flakes; cook and stir 30 seconds.

2. Stir in jalapeño pepper and garlic. Add bell pepper and carrots; mix well. Add cauliflower; reduce heat to medium.

3. Stir in ¼ cup water; cook and stir until water evaporates. Add remaining ¼ cup water; cover and cook about 8 to 10 minutes or until vegetables are crisp-tender, stirring occasionally.

4. Add salt; mix well. Sprinkle with cilantro, if desired.

nutrients per serving (⅔ cup stir-fry): **40 Calories, 7g Carbohydrate, 1g Dietary Fiber, 1g Total Fat, <1g Saturated Fat, 0mg Cholesterol, 198mg Sodium, 2g Protein**

Indian-Style Vegetable Stir-Fry

refreshing
salads

Cucumber Tomato Salad
Makes 6 servings

½ cup rice vinegar*
3 tablespoons EQUAL® SPOONFUL**
3 cups unpeeled ¼-inch-thick sliced cucumbers, quartered (about
    2 medium)
2 cups chopped tomato (about 1 large)
½ cup chopped red onion
    Salt and pepper to taste

Distilled white vinegar can be substituted for rice vinegar.

**Can substitute 4½ packets Equal® sweetener.*

• Combine vinegar and Equal®. Add cucumbers, tomato and
onion. Season to taste with salt and pepper; mix well. Refrigerate,
covered, at least 30 minutes before serving.

*nutrients per serving (⅙ of total recipe (without
added salt and pepper)):* **26 Calories, 6g Carbohydrate,
1g Dietary Fiber, 0g Total Fat, 0g Saturated Fat, 0mg Cholesterol,
7mg Sodium, 1g Protein**

Cucumber Tomato Salad

Greens and Broccoli Salad with Peppy Vinaigrette

Makes 4 servings

4 sun-dried tomato halves (not packed in oil)
3 cups torn washed red-tipped or plain leaf lettuce
1½ cups broccoli florets
1 cup sliced fresh mushrooms
⅓ cup sliced radishes
2 tablespoons water
1 tablespoon balsamic vinegar
1 teaspoon vegetable oil
¼ teaspoon chicken bouillon granules
¼ teaspoon dried chervil leaves
¼ teaspoon dry mustard
⅛ teaspoon ground red pepper

1. Pour enough boiling water over tomatoes in small bowl to cover. Let stand 5 minutes; drain. Chop tomatoes. Combine tomatoes, lettuce, broccoli, mushrooms and radishes in large salad bowl.

2. Combine 2 tablespoons water, vinegar, oil, bouillon granules, chervil, mustard and ground red pepper in jar with tight-fitting lid. Cover; shake well. Add to salad; toss to combine.

nutrients per serving: 54 Calories, 9g Carbohydrate, 2g Dietary Fiber, 2g Total Fat, <1g Saturated Fat, 0mg Cholesterol, 79mg Sodium, 3g Protein

Greens and Broccoli Salad with Peppy Vinaigrette

Chicken Salad

Makes 4 servings

¼ cup *each* mayonnaise and sour cream
1 tablespoon lemon juice
1 teaspoon *each* sugar, grated lemon peel and Dijon mustard
½ teaspoon salt
⅛ to ¼ teaspoon white pepper
2 cups diced cooked chicken
1 cup sliced celery
¼ cup sliced green onions
  Lettuce leaves and crumbled blue cheese (optional)

Mix mayonnaise, sour cream, lemon juice, sugar, lemon peel, mustard, salt and pepper. Stir in chicken, celery and onions. Cover; chill 1 hour. Serve over lettuce and top with cheese, if desired.

nutrients per serving: 243 Calories, 4g Carbohydrate, 1g Dietary Fiber, 15g Total Fat, 4g Saturated Fat, 64mg Cholesterol, 473mg Sodium, 21g Protein

Cucumber and Onion Salad

Makes 6 (¾-cup) servings

2½ cups thinly sliced unpeeled cucumbers
½ cup thinly sliced onion
⅓ cup SPLENDA® No Calorie Sweetener, Granular
⅓ cup *each* white vinegar and water
¼ teaspoon salt
⅛ teaspoon black pepper

Layer cucumbers and onion in a non-metallic low-sided medium bowl. In a small bowl, combine SPLENDA® Granular, vinegar, water, salt, and pepper. Pour over vegetables. Cover; refrigerate at least 2 hours, stirring occasionally. Stir again just before serving.

nutrients per serving (¾ cup salad): 19 Calories, 5g Carbohydrate, <1g Dietary Fiber, <1g Total Fat, <1g Saturated Fat, 0mg Cholesterol, 100mg Sodium, <1g Protein

Chicken Salad

Scallop and Spinach Salad

Makes 4 servings

1 package (10 ounces) spinach leaves, washed, stemmed and torn
3 thin slices red onion, halved and separated
12 ounces sea scallops
⅛ teaspoon ground red pepper
⅛ teaspoon paprika
 Nonstick cooking spray
½ cup fat-free Italian salad dressing
¼ cup crumbled blue cheese
2 tablespoons toasted walnuts

1. Pat spinach dry; place in large bowl with red onion. Cover; set aside.

2. Rinse scallops. Cut in half horizontally (to make 2 thin rounds); pat dry. Sprinkle top sides lightly with red pepper and paprika. Spray large nonstick skillet with cooking spray; heat over high heat until very hot. Add half of scallops, seasoned sides down, in single layer, placing ½ inch or more apart. Sprinkle with red pepper and paprika. Cook 2 minutes or until browned on bottom. Turn scallops; cook 1 to 2 minutes or until opaque in center. Transfer to plate; cover to keep warm. Wipe skillet clean; repeat procedure with remaining scallops.

3. Place dressing in small saucepan; bring to a boil over high heat. Pour dressing over spinach and onion; toss to coat. Divide among 4 plates. Place scallops on top of spinach; sprinkle with blue cheese and walnuts.

nutrients per serving: 169 Calories, 6g Carbohydrate, 2g Dietary Fiber, 6g Total Fat, 2g Saturated Fat, 50mg Cholesterol, 660mg Sodium, 24g Protein

Scallop and Spinach Salad

Warm Roasted Vegetable Salad

Makes 6 servings

    4 cups broccoli florets
    2 red bell peppers, cut into ¼-inch-thick slices
    1 small red onion, cut into ¼-inch-thick slices
    1 small yellow onion, cut into ¼-inch-thick slices
1½ teaspoons olive oil
    1 tablespoon Dijon mustard
    1 tablespoon balsamic vinegar
    1 teaspoon hot pepper sauce
    ½ teaspoon salt
    ¼ cup chopped fresh basil

1. Preheat oven to 350°F. Combine broccoli, bell peppers, onions and oil in large casserole dish; toss to coat.

2. Bake vegetables 25 minutes, stirring occasionally.

3. Meanwhile, combine mustard, vinegar, hot pepper sauce and salt in small bowl with wire whisk until smooth. Stir mixture into hot vegetables; toss to coat. Sprinkle salad with basil; garnish, if desired. Serve warm.

nutrients per serving: 50 Calories, 8g Carbohydrate, 3g Dietary Fiber, 2g Total Fat, <1g Saturated Fat, 0mg Cholesterol, 8mg Sodium, 3g Protein

Warm Roasted Vegetable Salad

Grilled Shrimp over Greens

Makes 4 servings

¾ cup CARB OPTIONS™ Italian Dressing
1 pound uncooked medium shrimp, peeled and deveined
6 cups or 1 bag (10 ounces) mixed salad greens
¼ cup sliced radishes

1. In large, shallow nonaluminum baking dish, pour ¼ cup Carb Options Italian Dressing over shrimp; turn to coat. Cover and marinate in refrigerator, turning occasionally, up to 1 hour.

2. Remove shrimp from marinade, discarding marinade. Grill or broil shrimp, turning once and brushing with additional ¼ cup Dressing until shrimp turn pink.

3. To serve, toss remaining ¼ cup Dressing with greens and arrange on serving platter. Top with grilled shrimp and radishes.

Preparation Time: 10 minutes
Marinate Time: 1 hour
Cook Time: 5 minutes

nutrients per serving: 210 Calories, 2g Carbohydrate, 1g Dietary Fiber, 13g Total Fat, 2g Saturated Fat, 175mg Cholesterol, 730mg Sodium, 20g Protein

Low-Carb Taco Salad Supreme

Makes 4 servings

1 pound ground beef
½ cup chopped onion
2 cloves garlic, minced
1 teaspoon ground cumin
1 teaspoon chili powder
½ teaspoon salt
½ cup salsa, divided
6 cups packed torn or sliced romaine lettuce
1 large tomato, chopped
1 cup (4 ounces) shredded Mexican cheese blend or taco cheese, divided
2 tablespoons canola oil
1 ripe avocado, peeled, seeded and diced
¼ cup sour cream

1. Brown ground beef with onion in large skillet; pour off drippings. Add garlic, cumin, chili powder and salt; cook 1 minute, stirring frequently. Stir in ¼ cup salsa; cook and stir 1 minute. Remove from heat.

2. Combine lettuce, tomato and ½ cup cheese in large bowl. Combine remaining ¼ cup salsa and oil in small bowl. Add salsa mixture to salad; toss well. Divide salad among 4 serving plates. Spoon meat mixture evenly over salad; top with remaining ½ cup cheese, avocado and sour cream.

> *nutrients per serving (2 cups salad, ²/₃ cup meat mixture, 2 tablespoons cheese and 1 tablespoon sour cream):* **584 Calories, 11g Carbohydrate, 5g Dietary Fiber, 47g Total Fat, 17g Saturated Fat, 113mg Cholesterol, 668mg Sodium, 30g Protein**

Thai Broccoli Salad

Makes 4 servings

¼ cup creamy or chunky peanut butter
2 tablespoons EQUAL® SPOONFUL*
1½ tablespoons hot water
1 tablespoon lime juice
1 tablespoon light soy sauce
1½ teaspoons dark sesame oil
¼ teaspoon red pepper flakes
2 tablespoons vegetable oil
3 cups fresh broccoli florets
½ cup chopped red bell pepper
¼ cup sliced green onions
1 clove garlic, crushed

*May substitute 3 packets Equal® sweetener.

• Combine peanut butter, Equal®, hot water, lime juice, soy sauce, sesame oil and red pepper flakes until well blended; set aside.

• Heat vegetable oil in large skillet over medium-high heat. Add broccoli, red pepper, green onions and garlic. Stir-fry 3 to 4 minutes until vegetables are tender-crisp. Remove from heat and stir in peanut butter mixture.

• Serve warm or at room temperature.

nutrients per serving (¼ of total recipe):
204 Calories, 10g Carbohydrate, 4g Dietary Fiber, 17g Total Fat, 3g Saturated Fat, 0mg Cholesterol, 223mg Sodium, 7g Protein

Thai Broccoli Salad

Easy Greek Salad

Makes 6 servings

6 leaves Romaine lettuce, torn into 1½-inch pieces
1 cucumber, peeled and sliced
1 tomato, chopped
½ cup sliced red onion
⅓ cup (1 ounce) crumbled feta cheese
2 tablespoons extra-virgin olive oil
2 tablespoons lemon juice
1 teaspoon dried oregano leaves
½ teaspoon salt

1. Combine lettuce, cucumber, tomato, onion and cheese in large serving bowl.

2. Whisk together oil, lemon juice, oregano and salt in small bowl. Pour over lettuce mixture; toss until coated. Serve immediately.

Prep Time: 10 minutes

Serving Suggestion: This simple but delicious salad makes a great accompaniment for grilled steaks or chicken.

nutrients per serving: 71 Calories, 5g Carbohydrate, 1g Dietary Fiber, 6g Total Fat, 1g Saturated Fat, 4mg Cholesterol, 249mg Sodium, 1g Protein

Easy Greek Salad

Grilled Beef Salad

Makes 4 servings

½ cup mayonnaise
2 tablespoons cider vinegar or white wine vinegar
1 tablespoon spicy brown mustard
2 cloves garlic, minced
½ teaspoon sugar
6 cups torn assorted lettuces such as romaine, red leaf and Bibb
1 large tomato, seeded and chopped
⅓ cup chopped fresh basil
2 slices red onion, separated into rings
1 boneless beef top sirloin steak (about 1 pound)
½ teaspoon salt
½ teaspoon black pepper
½ cup herb or garlic croutons
　Additional black pepper (optional)

1. Prepare grill for direct cooking. Combine mayonnaise, vinegar, mustard, garlic and sugar in small bowl; mix well. Cover and refrigerate until serving.

2. Toss together lettuce, tomato, basil and onion in large bowl; cover and refrigerate until serving.

3. Sprinkle both sides of steak with salt and ½ teaspoon black pepper. Place steak on grid. Grill, uncovered, over medium heat 13 to 16 minutes for medium-rare to medium or until desired doneness, turning once.

4. Transfer steak to carving board. Slice in half lengthwise; carve crosswise into thin slices.

5. Add steak and croutons to bowl with lettuce mixture; toss well. Add mayonnaise mixture; toss until well coated. Serve with additional black pepper, if desired.

nutrients per serving: 405 Calories, 11g Carbohydrate, 3g Dietary Fiber, 28g Total Fat, 5g Saturated Fat, 80mg Cholesterol, 634mg Sodium, 27g Protein

Grilled Beef Salad

Crab Spinach Salad with Tarragon Dressing

Makes 4 servings

12 ounces coarsely flaked cooked crabmeat *or* 2 packages (6 ounces
    each) frozen crabmeat, thawed and drained
1 cup chopped tomatoes
1 cup sliced cucumber
⅓ cup sliced red onion
¼ cup fat-free salad dressing or mayonnaise
¼ cup reduced-fat sour cream
¼ cup chopped fresh parsley
2 tablespoons fat-free (skim) milk
2 teaspoons chopped fresh tarragon *or* ½ teaspoon dried tarragon
    leaves
1 clove garlic, minced
¼ teaspoon hot pepper sauce
8 cups torn washed stemmed spinach

1. Combine crabmeat, tomatoes, cucumber and onion in medium
bowl. Combine salad dressing, sour cream, parsley, milk, tarragon,
garlic and hot pepper sauce in small bowl.

2. Line four salad plates with spinach. Place crabmeat mixture
on spinach; drizzle with dressing.

> *nutrients per serving (1 cup salad with*
> *1½ tablespoons dressing and 2 cups spinach):*
> 170 Calories, 14g Carbohydrate, 4g Dietary Fiber, 4g Total Fat,
> <1g Saturated Fat, 91mg Cholesterol, 481mg Sodium, 22g Protein

Crab Spinach Salad with Tarragon Dressing

Curried Chicken & Zucchini Salad

Makes 4 servings

½ cup nonfat plain yogurt
⅓ cup mayonnaise
2 tablespoons chili sauce
1 teaspoon white wine vinegar
1 teaspoon grated onion
¾ teaspoon curry powder
¼ teaspoon salt
2 cups shredded cooked chicken
1 cup seedless red grapes
1 medium zucchini, cut into matchstick-size strips
   Leaf lettuce
¼ cup slivered almonds, toasted (see Tip)

1. Combine yogurt, mayonnaise, chili sauce, vinegar, onion, curry powder and salt in large bowl; stir until smooth. Add chicken, grapes and zucchini; toss to coat.

2. Arrange lettuce on plate. Top with chicken mixture; sprinkle with almonds.

Tip: To toast almonds, spread in single layer on baking sheet. Bake at 350°F about 6 minutes or until golden brown, stirring frequently.

nutrients per serving: 370 Calories, 12g Carbohydrate, 1g Dietary Fiber, 21g Total Fat, 4g Saturated Fat, 86mg Cholesterol, 300mg Sodium, 30g Protein

Curried Chicken & Zucchini Salad

Japanese Petal Salad
Makes 4 servings

1 pound medium shrimp, cooked *or* 2 cups chicken, cooked and
   shredded
   Romaine lettuce leaves
2 fresh California Nectarines, halved, pitted and thinly sliced
2 cups sliced cucumber
2 celery stalks, cut into 3-inch-matchstick pieces
⅓ cup shredded red radishes
   Sesame Dressing (recipe follows) or low calorie dressing
2 teaspoons sesame seeds (optional)

Center shrimp on 4 lettuce-lined salad plates. Fan nectarines to
right side of shrimp; overlap cucumber slices to left side. Place
celery at top of plate; mound radishes at bottom of plate. Prepare
dressing; pour 3 tablespoons over each salad. Sprinkle with sesame
seeds, if desired.

Sesame Dressing: In small bowl, combine ½ cup rice wine
vinegar (not seasoned type), 2 tablespoons reduced-sodium soy
sauce, 2 teaspoons sugar and 2 teaspoons dark sesame oil. Stir
until sugar is dissolved.

Favorite recipe from **California Tree Fruit Agreement**

> *nutrients per serving (¼ of total recipe):*
> **192 Calories, 15g Carbohydrate, 2g Dietary Fiber, 4g Total Fat,
> 1g Saturated Fat, 222mg Cholesterol, 573mg Sodium, 25g Protein**

Japanese Petal Salad

Oriental Steak Salad

Makes 4 servings

1 package (3 ounces) Oriental flavor instant ramen noodles, uncooked
4 cups water
1 bag (16 ounces) BIRDS EYE® frozen Farm Fresh Mixtures
    Cauliflower, Carrots & Snow Pea Pods
2 tablespoons vegetable oil
1 pound boneless beef top loin steak, cut into thin strips
⅓ cup Oriental sesame salad dressing
¼ cup chow mein noodles
    Lettuce leaves

• Reserve seasoning packet from noodles.

• In large saucepan, bring water to boil. Add ramen noodles and vegetables; return to boil and cook 5 minutes, stirring occasionally. Drain.

• Heat oil in large nonstick skillet over medium-high heat. Add beef; cook and stir about 8 minutes or until browned.

• Stir in reserved seasoning packet until beef is well coated.

• In large bowl, toss together beef, vegetables, ramen noodles and salad dressing. Sprinkle with chow mein noodles. Serve over lettuce.

Prep Time: 10 minutes
Cook Time: 12 to 15 minutes

Serving Suggestion: This salad also can be served chilled. Moisten with additional salad dressing, if necessary. Sprinkle with chow mein noodles and spoon over lettuce just before serving.

nutrients per serving: 449 Calories, 14g Carbohydrate,
3g Dietary Fiber, 28g Total Fat, 6g Saturated Fat,
90mg Cholesterol, 389mg Sodium, 36g Protein

Oriental Steak Salad

Crab Cobb Salad

Makes 8 servings

12 cups washed and torn romaine lettuce
2 cans (6 ounces each) crabmeat, drained
2 cups diced ripe tomatoes or halved cherry tomatoes
¼ cup (1½ ounces) crumbled blue or Gorgonzola cheese
¼ cup cholesterol-free bacon bits
¾ cup fat-free Italian or Caesar salad dressing
  Black pepper

1. Arrange lettuce on large serving platter. Arrange crabmeat, tomatoes, blue cheese and bacon bits in rows attractively over lettuce.

2. Just before serving, drizzle dressing evenly over salad. Sprinkle with pepper to taste. Toss well.

nutrients per serving: 110 Calories, 8g Carbohydrate, 2g Dietary Fiber, 3g Total Fat, 1g Saturated Fat, 46mg Cholesterol, 666mg Sodium, 12g Protein

Chunky Chicken Salad

Makes 4 servings

½ cup CARB OPTIONS™ Whipped Dressing
2 tablespoons chopped red onions
2 tablespoons chopped red and/or yellow bell peppers
2 tablespoons chopped celery
4 cups cut-up cooked chicken or turkey

1. In medium bowl, combine all ingredients. Season, if desired, with salt and ground black pepper. Chill, if desired, and garnish with chopped green onions.

nutrients per serving: 370 Calories, 2g Carbohydrate, 0g Dietary Fiber, 21g Total Fat, 5g Saturated Fat, 140mg Cholesterol, 330mg Sodium, 41g Protein

Crab Cobb Salad

Salmon Broccoli Waldorf Salad

Makes 4 servings

1 bag (16 ounces) BIRDS EYE® frozen Broccoli Cuts
1 large Red Delicious apple, chopped
¼ cup thinly sliced green onions
½ cup bottled creamy roasted garlic, ranch or blue cheese dressing
1 can (14¾ ounces) salmon, drained and flaked

• In large saucepan, cook broccoli according to package directions; drain and rinse under cold water in colander.

• In large bowl, toss together broccoli, apple, onions and dressing. Gently stir in salmon; add pepper to taste.

Prep Time: 5 minutes
Cook Time: 7 minutes

Serving Suggestion: Serve over lettuce leaves and sprinkle with toasted nuts.

Birds Eye Idea: To prevent cut fruits and vegetables, such as apples, from discoloring, try rubbing them with a lemon wedge.

nutrients per serving: 389 Calories, 13g Carbohydrate, 4g Dietary Fiber, 17g Total Fat, 4g Saturated Fat, 58mg Cholesterol, 964mg Sodium, 23g Protein

Salmon Broccoli Waldorf Salad

Beef Salad

Makes 4 (13-ounce) servings

Dressing

- 1 container (6 ounces) plain non-fat yogurt
- 1 tablespoon water
- 2 teaspoons minced fresh onion
- 1 teaspoon minced fresh garlic
- ½ teaspoon salt
- ¼ teaspoon celery seed
- ¼ teaspoon pepper

Salad

- PAM® No-Stick Cooking Spray
- 1 package (6 ounces) frozen pea pods, thawed and drained
- 1 cup onion, sliced into rings
- 12 ounces cooked lean beef, cut in julienne strips
- 1 tomato cut in thin wedges
- 1 head butter lettuce, washed and drained

Dressing

1. In small bowl, combine *all* dressing ingredients; mix well. Set aside.

Salad

2. Spray skillet with PAM® Cooking Spray. Sauté pea pods and onion until tender. Remove from heat.

3. In bowl, combine pea pod mixture, beef, and tomato; chill.

4. Serve on bed of lettuce with dressing.

Serving Suggestion: You can substitute any lean meat, poultry or fish for the beef.

nutrients per serving (¼ of total recipe):
250 Calories, 13g Carbohydrate, 3g Dietary Fiber, 8g Total Fat,
3g Saturated Fat, 74mg Cholesterol, 389mg Sodium, 31g Protein

Seafood Salad

Makes 6 servings

4 tablespoons olive oil, divided
½ cup diced onion
2 cloves garlic, minced
8 ounces medium shrimp, peeled, deveined
8 ounces medium scallops
¼ teaspoon salt
¼ teaspoon ground black pepper
1 cup Italian bread cubes
1 can (14.5 ounces) CONTADINA® Recipe Ready Diced Tomatoes, drained
2 cups torn salad greens
1 cup yellow bell pepper, cut into strips
2 tablespoons chopped fresh Italian parsley
1 tablespoon white wine vinegar

1. Heat 1 tablespoon oil in medium skillet. Add onion and garlic; sauté for 1 minute.

2. Add shrimp, scallops, salt and black pepper; sauté for 3 minutes. Remove from heat.

3. Heat 1 tablespoon oil in small skillet. Add bread cubes; sauté until golden brown.

4. Toss seafood mixture, tomatoes, greens, bell pepper, parsley, remaining oil and vinegar in large bowl. Top with bread cubes.

Prep Time: 10 minutes
Cook Time: 10 minutes

nutrients per serving (⅙ of total recipe):
207 Calories, 11g Carbohydrate, 2g Dietary Fiber, 11g Total Fat,
1g Saturated Fat, 70mg Cholesterol, 573mg Sodium, 16g Protein

incredible
entrées

Moroccan-Style Lamb Chops
Makes 4 servings

    1 tablespoon olive oil
    1 teaspoon ground cumin
    1 teaspoon ground coriander
    ¾ teaspoon salt
    ⅛ teaspoon ground cinnamon
    ⅛ teaspoon ground red pepper
    4 center cut loin lamb chops, cut 1 inch thick (about 1 pound total)
    2 cloves garlic, minced

Prepare grill or preheat broiler. Combine oil, cumin, coriander, salt, cinnamon and red pepper in small bowl; mix well. Rub or brush oil mixture over both sides of lamb chops. Sprinkle garlic over both sides of lamb chops. Grill on covered grill, or broil 4 to 5 inches from heat, 5 minutes per side for medium doneness.

Hint: This recipe also works well with an indoor countertop grill.

nutrients per serving: 173 Calories, <1g Carbohydrate, <1g Dietary Fiber, 8g Total Fat, 2g Saturated Fat, 71mg Cholesterol, 510mg Sodium, 23g Protein

Moroccan-Style Lamb Chop

Sausage and Chicken Gumbo

Makes 6 servings

1 tablespoon canola oil
1 red bell pepper, chopped
1 pound boneless skinless chicken thigh meat, trimmed of excess fat
  and cut into 1-inch pieces
1 package (12 ounces) chicken sausage in Cajun andouille or chili
  flavor, sliced ½ inch thick
½ cup chicken broth
1 can (28 ounces) crushed tomatoes with roasted garlic
1 bay leaf
½ teaspoon dried basil leaves
¼ cup finely chopped green onions
½ teaspoon black pepper
¼ to ½ teaspoon red pepper flakes
6 lemon wedges

1. Heat oil in large saucepan. Add bell pepper; cook and stir over high heat 2 to 3 minutes. Add chicken; cook and stir about 2 minutes or until browned. Add sausage; cook and stir 2 minutes or until browned. Add chicken broth; scrape up any browned bits from bottom of saucepan.

2. Add tomatoes, bay leaf, basil, green onions, black pepper and red pepper flakes. Simmer 15 minutes. Remove and discard bay leaf. Garnish each serving with lemon wedge.

nutrients per serving (1⅓ cups gumbo):
239 Calories, 10g Carbohydrate, 2g Dietary Fiber, 11g Total Fat,
2g Saturated Fat, 103mg Cholesterol, 1000mg Sodium,
28g Protein

Sausage and Chicken Gumbo

Bacon-Cheese Burgers with Orange Salsa

Makes 4 servings

2 large oranges, peeled, pith removed and diced
1 jalapeño pepper,* seeded and finely chopped
1 large shallot, peeled and finely chopped
1 tablespoon minced fresh cilantro
1 teaspoon cider vinegar
1 teaspoon honey
¼ teaspoon salt
4 slices bacon
1 pound ground beef round
½ cup (2 ounces) shredded sharp Cheddar cheese

Jalapeño peppers can sting and irritate the skin; wear rubber gloves when handling peppers and do not touch eyes. Wash hands after handling.

1. For orange salsa, combine oranges, jalapeño, shallot, cilantro, cider vinegar, honey and salt in medium bowl. Stir until well blended; set aside.

2. Cook bacon in large skillet until very crisp. Drain on paper towels; crumble or chop into small pieces. Discard all but 1 tablespoon bacon drippings from skillet.

3. Combine bacon, beef and cheese in large bowl; stir gently until just mixed. Shape into 4 patties. Cook in bacon drippings remaining in skillet about 5 minutes per side or until well browned and no longer pink in center. Serve with orange salsa.

nutrients per serving (1 burger with ½ cup salsa):
285 Calories, 10g Carbohydrate, 2g Dietary Fiber, 13g Total Fat, 6g Saturated Fat, 86mg Cholesterol, 389mg Sodium, 31g Protein

Bacon-Cheese Burger with Orange Salsa

Szechwan Seafood Stir-Fry

Makes 4 servings

1 package (10 ounces) fresh spinach leaves
4 teaspoons dark sesame oil, divided
4 cloves garlic, minced and divided
¼ cup reduced-sodium soy sauce
1 tablespoon cornstarch
1 tablespoon dry sherry or sake
1 medium red bell pepper, cut into thin 1-inch-long strips
1½ teaspoons minced fresh or bottled gingerroot
¾ pound peeled deveined large raw shrimp, thawed if frozen
½ pound fresh bay scallops
2 teaspoons sesame seeds, toasted

1. Rinse spinach in cold water; drain. Heat 2 teaspoons oil in large saucepan over medium heat. Add 2 cloves garlic; stir-fry 1 minute. Add spinach; cover and steam 4 to 5 minutes or until spinach is wilted, turning with tongs after 3 minutes. Remove from heat; keep covered.

2. Meanwhile, combine soy sauce, cornstarch and sherry; stir until smooth. Set aside. Heat remaining 2 teaspoons oil in large nonstick skillet over medium-high heat. Add bell pepper; stir-fry 2 minutes. Add remaining 2 cloves garlic and ginger; stir-fry 1 minute. Add shrimp; stir-fry 2 minutes. Add scallops; stir-fry 1 minute or until shrimp and scallops are opaque and cooked through. Add soy sauce mixture; stir-fry 1 minute or until sauce thickens.

3. Stir spinach mixture and transfer to 4 individual plates; top with seafood mixture and sprinkle with sesame seeds.

Tip: Larger, less expensive sea scallops can be substituted for the bay scallops; simply cut them into quarters.

nutrients per serving: 249 Calories, 10g Carbohydrate, 7g Dietary Fiber, 9g Total Fat, 1g Saturated Fat, 147mg Cholesterol, 960mg Sodium, 31g Protein

Szechwan Seafood Stir-Fry

Pork & Peppers Mexican-Style

Makes 4 servings

2 tablespoons olive oil
½ cup chopped green onions
¾ pound lean pork, cut into ¼-inch pieces
3 bell peppers, preferably red, green and yellow, diced (about 2 cups)
1 teaspoon minced garlic
  Salt and black pepper
1 cup sliced fresh mushrooms
1 teaspoon cumin
1 teaspoon chili powder
½ teaspoon ground dried chipotle pepper (optional)
¼ cup shredded Cheddar cheese
¼ cup sour cream

1. Heat oil in large skillet over medium high heat. Add green onions; cook and stir 2 minutes. Add pork; cook and stir 5 minutes or until browned. Add bell peppers and garlic. Cook and stir 5 minutes or until bell peppers begin to soften.

2. Season with salt and pepper. Add mushrooms, cumin, chili powder and chipotle pepper, if desired. Cook and stir 10 to 15 minutes or until pork is cooked through and vegetables are tender.

3. Top each serving with shredded cheese and sour cream.

Tip: Those not restricting carbohydrates can enjoy this dish rolled-up in tortillas, burrito-style.

nutrients per serving: **271 Calories, 9g Carbohydrate, 3g Dietary Fiber, 17g Total Fat, 6g Saturated Fat, 63mg Cholesterol, 98mg Sodium, 22g Protein**

Pork & Peppers Mexican-Style

Steaks with Creamy Mushroom Sauce

Makes 4 servings

4 boneless sirloin steaks (about 6 ounces each)
2 tablespoons BERTOLLI® Classico Olive Oil
1 medium onion, finely chopped
1 package (10 ounces) mushrooms, thinly sliced
1 jar (1 pound) CARB OPTIONS™ Alfredo Sauce
2 teaspoons chopped fresh thyme leaves (optional)

1. Season steaks, if desired, with salt and ground black pepper. Grill or broil steaks until desired doneness.

2. Meanwhile, in 12-inch nonstick skillet, heat olive oil over medium-high heat and cook onion, stirring occasionally, 2 minutes or until tender. Add mushrooms and cook, stirring frequently, 5 minutes or until mushrooms are tender. Stir in Carb Options Alfredo Sauce and thyme and simmer 3 minutes or until heated through. Serve creamy mushroom sauce over steaks.

Preparation Time: 10 minutes
Cook Time: 15 minutes

nutrients per serving: 490 Calories, 10g Carbohydrate, 2g Dietary Fiber, 39g Total Fat, 13g Saturated Fat, 55mg Cholesterol, 780mg Sodium, 25g Protein

Microwaved Lemon-Apple Fish Rolls
Makes 4 servings

4 sole, cod or red snapper fillets (1 pound)
   Grated peel of 1 SUNKIST® lemon, divided
1 teaspoon dried dill weed, divided
¾ cup plus 2 tablespoons apple juice, divided
   Juice of ½ SUNKIST® lemon
2 tablespoons finely minced onion
1 tablespoon unsalted margarine
1 tablespoon all-purpose flour
1 tablespoon chopped parsley

Sprinkle fish with half the lemon peel and half the dill. Roll up each fillet; place, seam-side-down, in 8-inch round microwavable dish. Combine ¼ cup apple juice, lemon juice, onion, remaining lemon peel and dill; pour over fish. Dot with margarine. Cover with vented plastic wrap. Microwave at HIGH 3 minutes. Uncover; spoon cooking liquid over fish. Cook, covered, 3 to 4 minutes or until fish flakes easily with fork. Let stand, covered, while making sauce.

Pour cooking liquid from fish into small microwavable bowl. Blend remaining 2 tablespoons apple juice into flour; stir into cooking liquid. Microwave at HIGH 3 to 4 minutes; stir twice until sauce boils and thickens slightly. Add parsley; spoon over fish.

nutrients per serving: **167 Calories, 9g Carbohydrate,**
<1g Dietary Fiber, 4g Total Fat, 1g Saturated Fat,
60mg Cholesterol, 95mg Sodium, 22g Protein

Chicken with Herbed Cheese

Makes 4 servings

1 tablespoon butter
2 cups chopped fresh shiitake mushrooms
1 shallot, minced
¼ teaspoon dried thyme leaves
½ teaspoon salt, divided
½ teaspoon black pepper, divided
¼ cup half-and-half
¼ cup chicken broth
4 boneless skinless chicken breasts, pounded or sliced ¼ inch thick
¼ cup reduced-fat garlic-and-herb spreadable cheese
4 thin slices (4 ounces) ham
¼ cup chicken broth
1 tablespoon minced Italian parsley

1. Preheat oven to 350°F. Melt butter in medium skillet. Add mushrooms, shallot, thyme, ¼ teaspoon salt and ¼ teaspoon pepper. Cook over medium heat 5 minutes or until mushrooms are tender. Add half-and-half and broth; simmer 5 minutes or until slightly thickened. Pour half of mixture into shallow ovenproof dish. Set remainder aside.

2. Place chicken breasts on work surface. Spread 1 tablespoon cheese down center of each breast. Top with 1 ham slice. Roll up; place chicken seam-side down over mushroom mixture in dish. Sprinkle with remaining ¼ teaspoon salt and ¼ teaspoon pepper. Top with remaining mushroom mixture. Bake 20 to 25 minutes or until cooked through. Sprinkle with Italian parsley.

nutrients per serving: 274 Calories, 13g Carbohydrate, 2g Dietary Fiber, 9g Total Fat, 4g Saturated Fat, 100mg Cholesterol, 989mg Sodium, 36g Protein

Chicken with Herbed Cheese

Maryland Crab Cakes

Makes 6 servings

1 pound fresh backfin crabmeat, cartilage removed
10 reduced-sodium crackers (2 inches each), crushed to equal ½ cup
    crumbs
1 rib celery, finely chopped
1 green onion, finely chopped
¼ cup cholesterol-free egg substitute
3 tablespoons fat-free tartar sauce
1 teaspoon seafood seasoning
    Nonstick cooking spray
2 teaspoons vegetable oil
    Lemon wedges or slices (optional)

1. Combine crabmeat, cracker crumbs, celery and onion in medium bowl; set aside.

2. Mix egg substitute, tartar sauce and seafood seasoning in small bowl; pour over crabmeat mixture. Gently mix so large lumps will not be broken. Shape into 6 (¾-inch-thick) patties. Cover; refrigerate 30 minutes.

3. Spray large skillet with cooking spray. Add oil; heat over medium-high heat. Place crab cakes in skillet; cook 3 to 4 minutes on each side or until cakes are lightly browned. Garnish with lemon wedges or slices, if desired.

nutrients per serving (1 crab cake without garnish): **127** Calories, **8g** Carbohydrate, **0g** Dietary Fiber, **4g** Total Fat, **0g** Saturated Fat, **44mg** Cholesterol, **382mg** Sodium, **14g** Protein

Maryland Crab Cakes

Parmesan Turkey Breast

Makes 4 servings

1 pound turkey breast or chicken breasts, cut ⅛ to ¼ inch thick
½ teaspoon salt
¼ teaspoon black pepper
2 tablespoons butter, melted
2 cloves garlic, minced
½ cup grated Parmesan cheese
1 cup marinara sauce, warmed
2 tablespoons chopped fresh basil

Preheat broiler. Sprinkle turkey with salt and pepper; place in single layer in 15×10-inch pan. Combine butter and garlic in small bowl; brush over turkey. Broil turkey 4 to 5 inches from heat 2 minutes; turn. Sprinkle with cheese. Broil 2 to 3 minutes or until turkey is no longer pink in center. Transfer to serving plates. Spoon sauce over turkey; sprinkle with basil.

nutrients per serving: 251 Calories, 5g Carbohydrate, 2g Dietary Fiber, 10g Total Fat, 6g Saturated Fat, 95mg Cholesterol, 832mg Sodium, 33g Protein

Buttery Pepper and Citrus Broiled Fish

Makes 4 servings

3 tablespoons MOLLY MCBUTTER® Flavored Sprinkles
1 tablespoon MRS. DASH® Lemon Pepper Blend
1 tablespoon lime juice
2 teaspoons honey
1 pound boneless white fish fillets

Combine first 4 ingredients in small bowl; mix well. Broil fish 6 to 8 inches from heat, turning once. Spread with Lemon Pepper mixture. Broil an additional 4 to 5 minutes.

nutrients per serving (1 fillet): 117 Calories, 6g Carbohydrate, 1g Dietary Fiber, 1g Total Fat, <1g Saturated Fat, 49mg Cholesterol, 424mg Sodium, 20g Protein

Parmesan Turkey Breast

Stuffed Flank Steak

Makes 6 servings

1 cup dry red wine
¼ cup soy sauce
2 cloves garlic, minced
1 large flank steak, 1½ to 2 pounds
1 cup thawed frozen chopped spinach, squeezed dry
1 jar (7 ounces) roasted red bell peppers, drained and chopped
½ cup crumbled blue cheese
   Salt and black pepper

1. Combine wine, soy sauce and garlic in small bowl. Place steak in large resealable plastic food storage bag; pour marinade over steak. Seal bag; marinate in refrigerator 2 hours.

2. Preheat oven to 350°F. Combine spinach, roasted peppers and cheese in medium bowl. Remove steak from marinade, reserving marinade. Pat steak dry and place on flat work surface.

3. Spoon spinach and pepper mixture lengthwise across ⅔ of steak. Roll steak tightly around vegetables, securing with toothpicks or string.

4. Season with salt and black pepper; place in roasting pan. Bake 30 to 40 minutes for medium-rare, or until desired degree of doneness is reached, basting twice with reserved marinade. Do not baste during last 10 minutes of cooking time. Allow steak to rest about 10 minutes; slice to serve.

nutrients per serving: 288 Calories, 7g Carbohydrate, 1g Dietary Fiber, 13g Total Fat, 6g Saturated Fat, 56mg Cholesterol, 990mg Sodium, 28g Protein

Stuffed Flank Steak

Turkey Teriyaki

Makes 4 servings

2 tablespoons low-sodium soy sauce
2 tablespoons cooking sherry or apple juice
1 tablespoon canola oil
1 teaspoon ground ginger
1 teaspoon packed light brown sugar
1 clove garlic, minced
½ teaspoon black pepper
1 pound turkey or chicken cutlets
    Additional canola oil (optional)

Combine all ingredients except turkey in small bowl; mix well. Place turkey in resealable plastic food storage bag. Pour soy sauce mixture over turkey; seal bag. Refrigerate several hours or overnight.

Remove turkey from bag; discard marinade. Grill 18 to 25 minutes or sauté in 1 teaspoon canola oil in skillet over medium heat until meat is no longer pink in center.

Favorite recipe from **Canada's Canola Industry**

nutrients per serving (¼ of total recipe):
184 Calories, 4g Carbohydrate, 1g Dietary Fiber, 1g Total Fat, <1g Saturated Fat, 88mg Cholesterol, 160mg Sodium, 37g Protein

Chicken-Asparagus Marsala

Makes 4 servings

4 boneless, skinless chicken breast halves
2 tablespoons butter or margarine
½ pound small mushrooms
¼ cup Marsala wine
¼ cup water
½ teaspoon salt
¼ teaspoon black pepper
1 pound fresh asparagus, cut into 5-inch spears*
1 tablespoon chopped parsley

1½ packages (10 ounces each) frozen asparagus spears can be substituted.

On hard surface with meat mallet or similar flattening utensil, pound chicken to ¼-inch thickness. In frypan, place butter or margarine; heat to medium-high temperature. Add chicken and cook, turning, about 5 minutes or until browned. Remove chicken and set aside. To drippings remaining in same frypan, add mushrooms and cook, stirring, about 2 minutes. Add Marsala wine, water, salt and pepper. Return chicken to pan; spoon sauce over chicken. Arrange asparagus over chicken. Heat to boiling; reduce heat to medium, cover and cook about 8 minutes or until chicken is fork tender. Transfer chicken and asparagus to serving platter; keep warm. Heat Marsala sauce to boiling and boil about 2 minutes to reduce liquid. Spoon sauce over chicken; sprinkle with chopped parsley.

Favorite recipe from **Delmarva Poultry Industry, Inc.**

nutrients per serving: **236 Calories, 8g Carbohydrate, 3g Dietary Fiber, 8g Total Fat, 3g Saturated Fat, 68mg Cholesterol, 424mg Sodium, 31g Protein**

Creamy Chile and Chicken Casserole

Makes 6 servings

 3 tablespoons butter, divided
 2 jalapeño peppers,* seeded and finely chopped
 2 tablespoons flour
 ½ cup heavy cream
 1 cup chicken broth
 1 cup (4 ounces) shredded sharp Cheddar cheese
 1 cup (4 ounces) shredded Asiago cheese
 1 rib celery, chopped
 1 cup sliced mushrooms
 1 yellow squash, chopped
 1 red bell pepper, chopped
12 ounces cooked diced chicken breast meat
 ¼ cup chopped green onions, including some green parts
 ¼ teaspoon *each* salt and black pepper
 ½ cup sliced bacon-Cheddar flavored almonds

*Jalapeño peppers can sting and irritate the skin; wear rubber gloves when handling peppers and do not touch eyes. Wash hands after handling.

1. Preheat oven to 350°F. Melt 2 tablespoons butter in medium saucepan. Add jalapeño peppers; cook and stir over high heat 1 minute. Add flour; stir to make paste. Add cream; stir until thickened. Add broth; stir until smooth. Gradually add cheeses, stirring to melt. Set aside.

2. Melt remaining 1 tablespoon butter in large skillet. Add celery, mushrooms, yellow squash and bell pepper. Cook and stir over high heat 3 to 5 minutes or until vegetables are tender. Remove from heat. Stir in chicken, green onions, salt and pepper. Stir in cheese sauce.

3. Spoon mixture into shallow 2-quart casserole dish. Sprinkle with sliced almonds. Bake 10 minutes or until casserole is bubbly and hot.

nutrients per serving: 464 Calories, 8g Carbohydrate, 2g Dietary Fiber, 35g Total Fat, 17g Saturated Fat, 121mg Cholesterol, 789mg Sodium, 30g Protein

Creamy Chile and Chicken Casserole

Grilled Red Snapper with Avocado-Papaya Salsa

Makes 4 servings

1 teaspoon ground coriander seed
1 teaspoon paprika
¾ teaspoon salt
⅛ to ¼ teaspoon ground red pepper
1 tablespoon olive oil
4 skinless red snapper or halibut fish fillets (5 to 7 ounces each)
½ cup diced ripe avocado
½ cup diced ripe papaya
2 tablespoons chopped fresh cilantro
1 tablespoon fresh lime juice
4 lime wedges

1. Prepare grill for direct grilling. Combine coriander, paprika, salt and red pepper in small bowl or cup; mix well.

2. Brush oil over fish. Sprinkle 2½ teaspoons spice mixture over fish fillets; set aside remaining spice mixture. Place fish on oiled grid over medium-hot heat. Grill 5 minutes per side or until fish is opaque.

3. Meanwhile, combine avocado, papaya, cilantro, lime juice and remaining spice mixture in medium bowl; mix well. Serve fish with salsa and garnish with lime wedges.

nutrients per serving: **221 Calories, 5g Carbohydrate, 2g Dietary Fiber, 9g Total Fat, <1g Saturated Fat, 51mg Cholesterol, 559mg Sodium, 30g Protein**

Grilled Red Snapper with Avocado-Papaya Salsa

Two-Cheese Sausage Pizza

Makes 4 servings

1 pound sweet Italian turkey sausage
1 tablespoon olive oil
1 small red onion, thinly sliced
2 cups sliced mushrooms
1 small green bell pepper, cut into thin strips
¼ teaspoon dried oregano leaves
¼ teaspoon salt
¼ teaspoon black pepper
½ cup pizza sauce
2 tablespoons tomato paste
½ cup shredded Parmesan cheese
1 cup shredded reduced-fat mozzarella cheese
8 pitted ripe olives

1. Preheat oven to 400°F. Remove sausage from casings. Pat into greased 9-inch glass pie plate. Bake 10 minutes or until sausage is firm. Remove from oven and carefully pour off fat. Set aside.

2. Heat oil in large skillet. Add onion, mushrooms, bell pepper, oregano, salt and black pepper. Cook and stir over medium-high heat 10 minutes or until vegetables are very tender and no longer give off any liquid.

3. Combine pizza sauce and tomato paste in small bowl; stir until well blended. Spread over sausage crust. Spoon half of vegetables over tomato sauce. Sprinkle with Parmesan and mozzarella cheeses. Top with remaining vegetables. Sprinkle with olives. Bake 8 to 10 minutes or until cheese melts.

nutrients per serving: 507 Calories, 11g Carbohydrate, 3g Dietary Fiber, 43g Total Fat, 15g Saturated Fat, 78mg Cholesterol, 1249mg Sodium, 27g Protein

Two-Cheese Sausage Pizza

Shrimp Scampi over Hot Tomato Relish

Makes 4 servings

Hot Tomato Relish (recipe follows)
¼ cup olive oil
1 tablespoon unsalted butter
1 large clove garlic, minced
1 pound large raw shrimp, peeled and deveined
1 tablespoon lemon juice
2 tablespoons minced Italian parsley
¼ teaspoon *each* salt and black pepper
4 lemon wedges

1. Prepare Hot Tomato Relish and set aside. Combine oil and butter in large skillet over very low heat. Add garlic and simmer 10 minutes; do not burn.

2. Add shrimp. Cook over low heat 5 minutes, turning once, or until shrimp are opaque and cooked through. Stir in lemon juice, parsley, salt and pepper. Serve over relish with lemon wedges.

Hot Tomato Relish

Makes 4 servings

1 tablespoon olive oil
2 cups halved grape tomatoes
¼ teaspoon salt
¼ teaspoon black pepper
1 tablespoon balsamic vinegar
1 tablespoon minced fresh basil

1. Heat olive oil in large skillet over high heat. Add tomatoes; cook 1 to 2 minutes or until tomatoes are hot, but not cooked through. Season with salt and pepper. Sprinkle with balsamic vinegar and basil before serving.

nutrients per serving (¼ of total recipe including ½ cup relish): **327** Calories, 9g Carbohydrate, 2g Dietary Fiber, 22g Total Fat, 5g Saturated Fat, 181mg Cholesterol, 470mg Sodium, 24g Protein

Shrimp Scampi over Hot Tomato Relish

Low-Carb Lasagna

Makes 15 servings

2 medium eggplants (about 1½ pounds total)
1 tablespoon plus 1 teaspoon salt, divided
1½ pounds ground beef
1½ cups meatless pasta sauce (8 or less grams of carbohydrate per ½ cup)*
1 teaspoon Italian seasoning
½ teaspoon garlic powder
½ teaspoon black pepper
4 cups (2 pounds) whole milk ricotta cheese
1 egg
3 tablespoons chopped fresh parsley, divided
2 cups (8 ounces) shredded mozzarella cheese
¼ cup grated Parmesan cheese

Check labels carefully. Carbohydrate counts vary greatly.

1. Preheat oven to 350°F. Grease 13×9-inch baking pan. Slice eggplants horizontally into ⅛-inch-thick pieces. Place in large colander; sprinkle with 1 tablespoon salt. Drain at least 20 minutes.

2. Meanwhile cook ground beef in large skillet until no longer pink. Drain fat. Add pasta sauce, Italian seasoning, remaining 1 teaspoon salt, garlic powder and pepper; cook and stir 5 minutes.

3. Spoon ricotta into large bowl. Add egg; beat at medium speed of electric mixer until light. Stir in 2 tablespoons parsley.

4. Rinse eggplant slices; pat dry with paper towels. Arrange single layer of eggplant slices in prepared pan. Layer with ½ of ricotta mixture, ½ of meat sauce, ½ of mozzarella and ½ of Parmesan. Arrange eggplant slices over top; layer with remaining ½ of ricotta mixture and ½ of meat sauce. Top with remaining eggplant slices, remaining mozzarella and Parmesan. Sprinkle with remaining 1 tablespoon parsley.

5. Bake uncovered 30 minutes. Tent loosely with foil and bake additional 10 minutes or until lasagna is heated through and sauce is bubbly.

nutrients per serving: 314 Calories, 9g Carbohydrate, 4g Dietary Fiber, 21g Total Fat, 11g Saturated Fat, 92mg Cholesterol, 494mg Sodium, 21g Protein

Mustard Grilled Chicken with Dipping Sauce
Makes 4 servings

½ cup CARB OPTIONS™ Whipped Dressing
2 green onions, chopped
2 tablespoons mustard
1 teaspoon apple cider vinegar
⅛ teaspoon ground black pepper
  Pinch salt
4 boneless, skinless chicken breast halves (about 1 pound)

1. In medium bowl, combine all ingredients except chicken. Reserve ⅓ cup mixture.

2. Grill or broil chicken, brushing frequently with remaining mixture, 12 minutes or until chicken is thoroughly cooked, turning once. Serve chicken with ⅓ cup reserved mixture and garnish, if desired, with additional chopped green onions.

Preparation Time: 10 minutes
Cook Time: 12 minutes

nutrients per serving: 240 Calories, 2g Carbohydrate, 0g Dietary Fiber, 14g Total Fat, 3g Saturated Fat, 80mg Cholesterol, 360mg Sodium, 25g Protein

Philly Cheese Steaks

Makes 4 servings

2 tablespoons canola oil, divided
1 green bell pepper
1 medium onion, peeled and thinly sliced
½ teaspoon salt, divided
½ teaspoon black pepper, divided
¼ teaspoon red pepper flakes (optional)
1 pound boneless beef rib-eye steaks, sliced ¼ inch thick
4 slices reduced-fat American cheese

1. Heat 1 tablespoon oil in large nonstick skillet. Add bell pepper and onion. Cook and stir over high heat 3 minutes or until tender. Sprinkle with ¼ teaspoon salt, ¼ teaspoon black pepper and red pepper flakes, if desired. Remove from skillet; set aside.

2. Heat remaining 1 tablespoon oil in skillet. Sprinkle steaks with remaining ¼ teaspoon salt and ¼ teaspoon black pepper.

3. Add steaks to skillet. Cook 2 minutes over high heat. Turn steaks; cook 1 minute or until desired degree of doneness. Cover each steak with 1 slice cheese. Heat 1 minute or until cheese melts.

4. Divide bell pepper mixture among 4 plates. Top each serving with 1 steak.

nutrients per serving: 294 Calories, 6g Carbohydrate, 1g Dietary Fiber, 16g Total Fat, 5g Saturated Fat, 64mg Cholesterol, 632mg Sodium, 30g Protein

Philly Cheese Steaks

Pork Tenderloin over Red Cabbage Slaw

Makes 4 servings

1 pork tenderloin (about 1 pound), trimmed of fat
1 large clove garlic, cut into thin slices
1 teaspoon dried oregano leaves
  Grated peel of 1 lemon
1 cup fat-free plain yogurt
¼ teaspoon *each* salt and black pepper
  Red Cabbage Slaw (recipe follows)

1. Pierce pork in several places with knife tip. Insert garlic slice, pinch of oregano and pinch of lemon peel. Place pork in bowl. Add yogurt; spread over all sides of pork to coat. Cover; refrigerate 4 to 6 hours. Remove pork from yogurt, scraping off any excess. Sprinkle pork with salt and pepper.

2. Preheat oven to 425°F. Place pork on shallow rack over roasting pan. Roast 45 minutes, turning over once, or until meat thermometer registers 160°F. Remove from heat. Slice ¼ inch thick on diagonal; serve with Red Cabbage Slaw.

Red Cabbage Slaw

Makes 2 cups

2 cups shredded red cabbage
½ cup chopped green onions, green parts only
2 tablespoons balsamic vinegar
1 tablespoon canola oil
1 teaspoon sugar
¼ teaspoon *each* salt and black pepper

Place cabbage and green onions in medium bowl; mix well. Combine vinegar, oil, sugar, salt and pepper in small bowl; stir until well blended. Pour over cabbage mixture; toss to coat.

nutrients per serving (¼ total pork tenderloin recipe plus ½ cup slaw): **222** Calories, **11g** Carbohydrate, **1g** Dietary Fiber, **7g** Total Fat, **2g** Saturated Fat, **74mg** Cholesterol, **389mg** Sodium, **28g** Protein

Pork Tenderloin over Red Cabbage Slaw

Tantalizing desserts

Berry Parfaits

Makes 4 (½-cup) servings

1 cup heavy cream
2 tablespoons sucralose-based sugar substitute
1 teaspoon grated lemon peel
½ teaspoon vanilla
¾ cup blueberries, divided
¾ cup sliced strawberries, divided
Lemon twist or fresh mint leaves (optional)

1. Beat cream, sugar substitute, lemon peel and vanilla in large bowl at high speed of electric mixer until thick.

2. Place 1 tablespoon blueberries and 1 tablespoon strawberries in each of 4 parfait or dessert dishes. Spoon ¼ cup cream mixture on top of berries. Repeat layers. Garnish with lemon twist or fresh mint leaves, if desired. Refrigerate until ready to serve.

Note: Frozen, unsweetened strawberries and/or blueberries can be substituted for the fresh berries. Thaw them before using.

nutrients per serving (½ cup): 235 Calories, 8g Carbohydrate, 1g Dietary Fiber, 22g Total Fat, 14g Saturated Fat, 82mg Cholesterol, 25mg Sodium, 2g Protein

Berry Parfaits

Flourless Chocolate Cake

Makes 12 servings

1 cup heavy cream
1 cup plus 2 tablespoons sucralose-based sugar substitute
12 squares (1 ounce each) unsweetened chocolate, coarsely chopped
4 squares (1 ounce each) semisweet chocolate, coarsely chopped
6 eggs, at room temperature
½ cup strong coffee
¼ teaspoon salt
½ cup chopped walnuts, divided
1 cup whipped cream (optional)

1. Preheat oven to 350°F; set oven rack to middle position. Spray 8-inch round cake pan with nonstick cooking spray.

2. Beat cream and 2 tablespoons sugar substitute in large bowl until soft peaks form; set aside.

3. Place unsweetened and semisweet chocolate in microwavable bowl; microwave at HIGH 2 to 3 minutes or until chocolate is melted, stirring at 30-second intervals after first minute.

4. Beat eggs and remaining 1 cup sugar substitute in large bowl about 7 minutes or until pale and thick. Add melted chocolate, coffee and salt to egg mixture; beat until well blended.

5. Fold whipped cream and ¼ cup walnuts into egg mixture. Spread in prepared pan; sprinkle with remaining ¼ cup walnuts. Place cake pan in large roasting pan; add enough hot water to roasting pan to reach halfway up side of cake pan. Bake 30 to 35 minutes or until set but still soft in center.

6. To unmold, loosen edge of cake with knife; place serving plate upside down over pan and invert. Serve warm garnished with whipped cream, if desired.

nutrients per serving: 320 Calories, 17g Carbohydrate,
6g Dietary Fiber, 30g Total Fat, 17g Saturated Fat,
134mg Cholesterol, 100mg Sodium, 8g Protein

Flourless Chocolate Cake

No-Bake Blueberry Cheesecake

Makes 8 servings

Crust
    8 zwieback toasts*
    1 tablespoon butter

Filling
    1 envelope (2½ teaspoons) unflavored gelatin
    1 cup boiling water
    2 packages (8 ounces each) cream cheese, softened
    ⅓ cup sucralose-based sugar substitute
    1 teaspoon vanilla
    1 cup thawed frozen whipped topping
    ¾ cup unsweetened frozen blueberries

Zwieback toast can be found in the baby food aisle of most grocery stores.

1. For crust, place zwieback toasts and 1 tablespoon butter in food processor; pulse until coarse crumbs form. Pat thin layer of crumbs on bottom of 9-inch springform pan.

2. Place gelatin in medium bowl. Add boiling water; stir until gelatin is completely dissolved.

3. Beat cream cheese, sugar substitute and vanilla in large bowl at medium speed of electric mixer until well blended. Beat in whipped topping. Add dissolved gelatin in steady stream while beating at low speed. (Mixture will become loose and lumpy.) Beat 4 minutes at medium speed until smooth and creamy, scraping side of bowl occasionally.

4. Fold frozen blueberries into cream cheese mixture; pour into prepared pan. Refrigerate 3 hours or until set.

nutrients per serving: 284 Calories, 11g Carbohydrate, 1g Dietary Fiber, 24g Total Fat, 15g Saturated Fat, 66mg Cholesterol, 196mg Sodium, 6g Protein

No-Bake Blueberry Cheesecake

Pineapple-Ginger Bavarian

Makes 5 servings

1 can (8 ounces) crushed pineapple in juice, drained and liquid
    reserved
1 package (4-serving size) sugar-free orange-flavored gelatin
1 cup sugar-free ginger ale
1 cup plain nonfat yogurt
¼ teaspoon grated fresh ginger
½ cup whipping cream
1 packet sugar substitute
¼ teaspoon vanilla

1. Combine reserved pineapple juice with enough water to equal
½ cup liquid. Pour into small saucepan. Bring to a boil over high
heat.

2. Place gelatin in medium bowl. Add pineapple juice mixture;
stir until gelatin is completely dissolved. Add ginger ale and half
of crushed pineapple; stir until well blended. Add yogurt; whisk
until well blended. Pour into 5 individual ramekins. Cover each
ramekin with plastic wrap; refrigerate until firm.

3. Meanwhile, combine remaining half of pineapple with ginger
in small bowl. Cover with plastic wrap; refrigerate.

4. Just before serving, beat cream in small deep bowl at high speed
of electric mixer until soft peaks form. Add sugar substitute and
vanilla; beat until stiff peaks form.

5. To serve, top each bavarian with 1 tablespoon whipped
cream and 1 tablespoon pineapple mixture.

> *nutrients per serving (1 bavarian):* **147** Calories,
> **12g** Carbohydrate, **<1g** Dietary Fiber, **9g** Total Fat, **6g** Saturated
> Fat, **34mg** Cholesterol, **111mg** Sodium, **4g** Protein

Pineapple-Ginger Bavarian

Chocolate Cannoli

Makes 8 servings

1 cup heavy cream
1 square (1 ounce) unsweetened chocolate
⅔ cup sucralose-based sugar substitute
⅓ cup whole milk ricotta cheese
1 teaspoon vanilla or almond extract
¼ teaspoon salt
8 unfilled cannoli shells (½ ounce each)*
1 teaspoon miniature chocolate chips or crushed pistachio nuts
   (optional)

Cannoli shells can be found at Italian bakeries and delis or in the ethnic food aisles at some supermarkets. If shells are unavailable, serve filling in dessert dish with sugar wafer or other cookie.

1. Beat cream in medium bowl at high speed of electric mixer until stiff peaks form. Set aside.

2. Place chocolate in small microwavable bowl; microwave at HIGH 1 to 2 minutes, stirring at 30-second intervals until chocolate is melted.

3. Combine sugar substitute, ricotta, vanilla and salt in medium bowl. Stir in melted chocolate. Fold whipped cream into mixture.

4. Spoon or pipe ¼ cup mixture into each cannoli shell. Garnish with chocolate chips or crushed pistachio nuts, if desired.

nutrients per serving (1 cannoli): 230 Calories, 12g Carbohydrate, 1g Dietary Fiber, 18g Total Fat, 10g Saturated Fat, 46mg Cholesterol, 23mg Sodium, 3g Protein

Chocolate Cannoli

Raspberry Cream Pie

Makes 8 servings

Crust

1⅓ cups ground pecans
2 tablespoons melted butter
1 tablespoon sucralose-based sugar substitute
¼ teaspoon ground cinnamon

Filling

½ cup water
1 envelope unflavored gelatin
6 tablespoons powdered sugar
¼ cup sucralose-based sugar substitute
1 tablespoon fresh lemon juice
⅛ teaspoon salt
2 cups fresh raspberries *or* 1 bag (12 ounces) frozen unsweetened
  raspberries, thawed
1 cup heavy cream

1. Preheat oven to 350°F. Combine ground pecans, melted butter, sugar substitute and cinnamon in medium bowl. Press onto bottom and up side of 9-inch pie plate. Bake 5 to 7 minutes or until crust is set and lightly browned. Cool completely.

2. Pour ½ cup water into medium saucepan; sprinkle with gelatin. Let stand 5 minutes or until gelatin is softened. Add powdered sugar, sugar substitute, lemon juice and salt. Cook and stir over medium-low heat until gelatin and sugar are dissolved. Stir in raspberries. Remove from heat; let stand about 30 minutes or until thickened.

3. Beat cream in medium bowl with electric mixer at high speed until stiff peaks form. Fold in raspberry mixture. Gently spoon into prepared crust. Refrigerate 2 to 3 hours before serving.

nutrients per serving: 299 Calories, 14g Carbohydrate,
4g Dietary Fiber, 27g Total Fat, 10g Saturated Fat,
49mg Cholesterol, 81mg Sodium, 3g Protein

Raspberry Cream Pie

Chocolate Cheesecake

Makes 10 servings

2 packages (8 ounces each) cream cheese, softened
2 eggs
⅓ cup plus 2 teaspoons sucralose-based sugar substitute, divided
2 tablespoons honey
3 teaspoons vanilla, divided
2 tablespoons unsweetened cocoa powder
1 cup heavy cream

1. Preheat oven to 350°F. Spray 8-inch round cake pan with nonstick cooking spray. Cut 8-inch parchment paper or wax paper circle to fit bottom of pan. Place paper in pan; spray lightly with cooking spray.

2. Beat cream cheese, eggs, ⅓ cup sugar substitute, honey and 2 teaspoons vanilla in large bowl with electric mixer at medium speed 2 to 3 minutes or just until well blended. With mixer running at low speed, beat in cocoa until well blended. *Do not overbeat.*

3. Pour batter into prepared pan. Bake 35 to 40 minutes or until center is set. Cool 10 minutes on wire rack; run thin knife around edge of cheesecake to loosen. Cool completely.

4. Invert cheesecake onto plate. Remove parchment paper. Place serving plate over cake; invert cake top side up. Cover loosely with plastic wrap. Refrigerate at least 4 hours or overnight.

5. Beat cream, remaining 2 teaspoons sugar substitute and 1 teaspoon vanilla in small deep bowl with electric mixer at high speed until stiff peaks form. Serve with cheesecake.

nutrients per serving (¹/₁₀ of cheesecake and 2 tablespoons whipped cream): 280 Calories, 7g Carbohydrate, <1g Dietary Fiber, 26g Total Fat, 16g Saturated Fat, 125mg Cholesterol, 158mg Sodium, 5g Protein

Chocolate Cheesecake

Cranberry Orange Cheesecake

Makes 16 servings

1⅓ cups gingersnap crumbs
3 tablespoons EQUAL® SPOONFUL*
3 tablespoons stick butter or margarine, melted
3 packages (8 ounces each) reduced-fat cream cheese, softened
1 cup EQUAL® SPOONFUL**
2 eggs
2 egg whites
2 tablespoons cornstarch
¼ teaspoon salt
1 cup reduced-fat sour cream
2 teaspoons vanilla
1 cup chopped fresh or frozen cranberries
1½ teaspoons grated orange peel

*May substitute 4½ packets Equal® sweetener.

**May substitute 24 packets Equal® sweetener.

• Mix gingersnap crumbs, 3 tablespoons Equal® and melted butter in bottom of 9-inch springform pan. Reserve 2 tablespoons crumb mixture. Pat remaining mixture evenly onto bottom of pan. Bake in preheated 325°F oven 8 minutes. Cool on wire rack.

• Beat cream cheese and 1 cup Equal® in large bowl until fluffy; beat in eggs, egg whites, cornstarch and salt. Beat in sour cream and vanilla until blended. Gently stir in cranberries and orange peel. Pour batter into crust in pan. Sprinkle with reserved crumb mixture.

• Bake in 325°F oven 45 to 50 minutes or until center is almost set. Remove cheesecake to wire rack. Gently run metal spatula around rim of pan to loosen cake. Let cheesecake cool completely; cover and refrigerate several hours or overnight before serving. To serve, remove sides of springform pan.

nutrients per serving: 193 Calories, 14g Carbohydrate,
1g Dietary Fiber, 11g Total Fat, 7g Saturated Fat,
57mg Cholesterol, 331mg Sodium, 7g Protein

Cranberry Orange Cheesecake

Strawberry Bavarian Deluxe

Makes 10 servings

½ bag whole frozen unsweetened strawberries (1 mounded quart),
    partially thawed
¼ cup low-sugar strawberry preserves
¼ cup granular sucralose
¾ cup water, divided
2 tablespoons balsamic vinegar
2 envelopes (7g each) unflavored gelatin
1 tablespoon honey
½ cup pasteurized liquid egg whites *or* 4 egg whites*
½ teaspoon cream of tartar
1 teaspoon vanilla
1 pint fresh strawberries, washed, dried and hulled
1 cup thawed frozen light whipped topping

Use clean, uncracked eggs

1. Place partially thawed strawberries, preserves and sucralose
in food processor fitted with steel blade; process until smooth.
Transfer mixture to large bowl. Set aside.

2. Combine ¼ cup water and vinegar in small saucepan;
sprinkle with gelatin. Let stand until softened. Stir in remaining
½ cup water and honey. Cook and stir over medium heat until
gelatin dissolves.

3. Whisk gelatin mixture into berry mixture in bowl.
Refrigerate, covered, until mixture is soupy, but not set.

4. Meanwhile, combine liquid egg whites, cream of tartar and
vanilla in large bowl. When berry-gelatin mixture is soupy, whip
egg white mixture until soft peaks form.

5. Gently fold egg whites, ⅓ at a time, into chilled gelatin mixture
until mixture is uniform in color. Pour mousse into prechilled
2-quart mold, such as nonstick Bundt pan. Refrigerate covered
for at least 8 hours or overnight.

6. To serve, run tip of knife around top of mold. Dip mold briefly into large bowl of hot water to loosen. To unmold, center flat serving plate on top of mold and holding firmly so mold doesn't shift, invert plate and mold. Shake gently to release. Remove mold; refrigerate bavarian 10 to 15 minutes. Cut into 10 wedges; serve with fresh strawberries and whipped topping.

nutrients per serving (1 wedge): 82 Calories, 15g Carbohydrate, 2g Dietary Fiber, 1g Total Fat, <1g Saturated Fat, 0mg Cholesterol, 25mg Sodium, 3g Protein

Nutty Cheesecake Bites
Makes 30 (¾-inch) servings

1 package (8 ounces) cream cheese, softened
½ cup CARB OPTIONS™ Creamy Peanut Spread
¼ cup SPLENDA® No Calorie Sweetener
¼ teaspoon ground cinnamon
¼ teaspoon vanilla extract
   Finely chopped peanuts or unsweetened shredded coconut

1. In medium bowl, with electric mixer on medium speed, combine all ingredients except peanuts, scraping down sides of bowl as needed. Chill 30 minutes or until firm.

2. Roll into ¾-inch balls, then roll in peanuts. Chill an additional 15 minutes before serving.

Preparation Time: 20 minutes
Chill Time: 45 minutes

nutrients per serving (1 cheesecake bite): 70 Calories, 2g Carbohydrate, 1g Dietary Fiber, 6g Total Fat, 3g Saturated Fat, 10mg Cholesterol, 40mg Sodium, 2g Protein

Raspberry Cheese Tarts

Makes 10 servings

Crust
1¼ cups graham cracker crumbs
5 tablespoons light margarine (50% less fat and calories)
¼ cup SPLENDA® No Calorie Sweetener, Granular

Filling
4 ounces reduced-fat cream cheese
½ cup plain nonfat yogurt
1 cup SPLENDA® Granular
½ cup egg substitute
1 cup frozen raspberries

Crust
1. Preheat oven to 350°F. In medium bowl, mix together graham cracker crumbs, margarine, and ¼ cup SPLENDA®. Press about 1 tablespoon of crust mixture into 10 muffin pan cups lined with paper liners. Set aside.

Filling
2. In small bowl, beat cream cheese with electric mixer on low speed until soft, about 30 seconds. Add yogurt and beat on low speed until smooth, approximately 1 minute. Stir in SPLENDA® and egg substitute until well blended.

3. Place 1½ tablespoons raspberries (4 to 5) into each muffin cup. Divide filling evenly among muffin cups. Bake for 20 minutes or until firm.

4. Refrigerate for 2 hours before serving. Garnish as desired.

Preparation Time: 25 minutes
Baking Time: 20 minutes
Chilling Time: 2 hours

> *nutrients per serving (1 tart or 2.6 ounces (82 g)):*
> 140 Calories, 15g Carbohydrate, 1g Dietary Fiber, 6g Total Fat,
> 2g Saturated Fat, 6mg Cholesterol, 255mg Sodium, 5g Protein

Raspberry Cheese Tarts

Coconut Flan

Makes 4 servings

3 tablespoons water
1 envelope unflavored gelatin
1 can (14½ ounces) unsweetened coconut milk
8 packets sucralose-based sugar substitute
2 tablespoons powdered sugar
½ teaspoon vanilla
4 tablespoons toasted flaked coconut
2 slices (½ inch thick) fresh pineapple, cut into bite-size pieces

1. Place water in small bowl and sprinkle with gelatin; set aside.

2. Place coconut milk, sugar substitute, powdered sugar and vanilla in medium saucepan. Heat over medium heat; stir to dissolve sugar and smooth out coconut milk. *Do not boil.* Add gelatin mixture; stir until gelatin is completely dissolved.

3. Pour coconut milk mixture evenly into four 5-ounce custard cups. Refrigerate about 3 hours or until set.

4. To unmold, run knife around outside edges of cups; place cups in hot water about 30 seconds. Place serving plate over cup; invert and shake until flan drops onto plate. Top each serving with 1 tablespoon toasted coconut and ¼ of pineapple pieces. Refrigerate leftovers.

Note: Flan is best eaten within 2 days.

nutrients per serving: 261 Calories, 13g Carbohydrate, 1g Dietary Fiber, 24g Total Fat, 21g Saturated Fat, 0mg Cholesterol, 18mg Sodium, 4g Protein

Coconut Flan

Chocolate Peanut Butter Ice Cream Sandwiches

Makes 4 servings

2 tablespoons creamy peanut butter
8 chocolate wafer cookies
⅔ cup no-sugar-added vanilla ice cream, softened

1. Spread peanut butter over flat sides of all cookies.

2. Spoon ice cream over peanut butter on 4 cookies. Top with remaining 4 cookies, peanut butter sides down. Press down lightly to force ice cream to edges of sandwich.

3. Wrap each sandwich in foil; seal tightly. Freeze at least 2 hours or up to 5 days.

nutrients per serving (1 sandwich): 129 Calories, 15g Carbohydrate, 1g Dietary Fiber, 7g Total Fat, 3g Saturated Fat, 4mg Cholesterol, 124mg Sodium, 4g Protein

Silky Peanutty Mousse

Makes 5 (½-cup) servings

1½ cups cold water
½ cup whipping or heavy cream
1 package (1 ounce) sugar free, fat free reduced calorie vanilla instant pudding
½ cup CARB OPTIONS™ Creamy Peanut Spread

1. In large bowl, combine water and cream. Add pudding and beat with wire whisk 2 minutes. Add Carb Options Creamy Peanut Spread and beat 1 minute or until thickened and smooth. Let stand 5 minutes or chill.

nutrients per serving (½ cup): 270 Calories, 8g Carbohydrate, 1g Dietary Fiber, 25g Total Fat, 11g Saturated Fat, 50mg Cholesterol, 300mg Sodium, 6g Protein

Chocolate Peanut Butter Ice Cream Sandwiches

Waist-Watcher's Cocoa Dessert

Makes 6 servings

1 envelope unflavored gelatin
1¾ cups cold water
⅔ cup nonfat dry milk powder
2 egg yolks, slightly beaten
3 tablespoons HERSHEY'S Cocoa
¼ teaspoon salt
½ cup sugar or equivalent amount of granulated sugar substitute
2 teaspoons vanilla extract
½ cup thawed frozen light non-dairy whipped topping
  Assorted fresh fruit, cut up (optional)
  Additional frozen light non-dairy whipped topping, thawed
    (optional)
  Additional HERSHEY'S Cocoa (optional)

1. Sprinkle gelatin over water in medium saucepan; let stand
5 minutes to soften. Add milk powder, egg yolks, 3 tablespoons
cocoa and salt. Cook over medium heat, stirring constantly, until
mixture begins to boil; remove from heat. Stir in sugar and vanilla.
Pour mixture into large bowl. Refrigerate, stirring occasionally,
until mixture mounds slightly when dropped from spoon, about
1 hour.

2. Fold ½ cup whipped topping into chocolate mixture. Pour
into 6 individual dessert dishes. Cover; refrigerate until firm,
about 4 hours. Garnish individual dessert dishes with assorted
fresh fruit or additional whipped topping, sprinkled with
additional cocoa, if desired.

Note: A 3-cup mold may be used in place of individual dessert
dishes, if desired.

*nutrients per serving (1 dish dessert (⅙ of total
recipe)):* 93 Calories, 11g Carbohydrate, 1g Dietary Fiber,
3g Total Fat, 1g Saturated Fat, 72mg Cholesterol, 144mg Sodium,
5g Protein

Waist-Watcher's Cocoa Dessert

Frozen Berry Ice Cream

Makes 8 (½-cup) servings

8 ounces frozen unsweetened strawberries, partially thawed
8 ounces frozen unsweetened peaches, partially thawed
4 ounces frozen unsweetened blueberries, partially thawed
6 packets sugar substitute
2 teaspoons vanilla
2 cups no-sugar-added light vanilla ice cream
16 blueberries
4 small strawberries, halved
8 peach slices

1. Combine partially thawed strawberries, peaches, blueberries, sugar substitute and vanilla in food processor. Process until coarsely chopped.

2. Add ice cream; process until well blended.

3. Serve immediately for semi-soft texture or freeze until ready to serve. (If frozen, let stand 10 minutes to soften slightly.) Garnish each serving with 2 blueberries for "eyes," 1 strawberry half for "nose" and 1 peach slice for "smile."

nutrients per serving (½ cup): **69 Calories, 15g Carbohydrate, 1g Dietary Fiber, <1g Total Fat, <1g Saturated Fat, 0mg Cholesterol, 23mg Sodium, 3g Protein**

Frozen Berry Ice Cream

Milk Chocolate Frozen Mousse

Makes 6 servings

1½ cups heavy cream, divided
½ cup water
1 envelope unflavored gelatin
2 tablespoons unsweetened cocoa powder
½ teaspoon ground cinnamon
6 tablespoons powdered sugar
¼ teaspoon salt
2 tablespoons sucralose-based sugar substitute
1 teaspoon vanilla
3 tablespoons honey-roasted sliced almonds

1. Combine ½ cup cream and water in small saucepan; sprinkle with gelatin. Let stand 5 minutes to soften. Stir in cocoa, cinnamon, powdered sugar and salt. Cook and stir over low heat until gelatin dissolves and mixture is well blended. Remove from heat; cool slightly. Stir in sugar substitute and vanilla.

2. Refrigerate gelatin mixture 1 hour or until partially set. Pour remaining 1 cup cream into large bowl. Beat at high speed of electric mixer until stiff peaks form. Gently fold chocolate mixture into cream. Spoon into 2-quart soufflé or casserole dish. Sprinkle with sliced almonds. Place in freezer 1 hour or until semi-frozen.

nutrients per serving (½ cup): **275** Calories, 12g Carbohydrate, 1g Dietary Fiber, 25g Total Fat, 14g Saturated Fat, 82mg Cholesterol, 129mg Sodium, 3g Protein

Milk Chocolate Frozen Mousse

Irresistible
cookies

Peanut Butter & Banana Cookies
Makes 2 dozen cookies

¼ cup (½ stick) butter
½ cup mashed ripe banana
½ cup no-sugar-added natural peanut butter
¼ cup thawed frozen unsweetened apple juice concentrate
 1 egg
 1 teaspoon vanilla
 1 cup all-purpose flour
½ teaspoon baking soda
¼ teaspoon salt
½ cup chopped salted peanuts
   Whole peanuts (optional)

Preheat oven to 375°F. Beat butter in large bowl until creamy. Add banana and peanut butter; beat until smooth. Blend in apple juice concentrate, egg and vanilla. Beat in flour, baking soda and salt. Stir in chopped peanuts. Drop rounded tablespoonfuls of dough 2 inches apart onto lightly greased cookie sheets; top each with one peanut, if desired. Bake 8 minutes or until set. Cool completely on wire racks. Store in tightly covered container.

nutrients per serving (1 cookie): **100 Calories, 9g Carbohydrate, 1g Dietary Fiber, 6g Total Fat, 2g Saturated Fat, 14mg Cholesterol, 88mg Sodium, 3g Protein**

Peanut Butter & Banana Cookies

Lip-Smacking Lemon Cookies

Makes about 4 dozen cookies

½ cup (1 stick) butter, softened
1 cup sugar
1 egg
2 tablespoons lemon juice
2 teaspoons grated lemon peel
2 cups all-purpose flour
1 teaspoon baking powder
⅛ teaspoon salt
   Dash ground nutmeg
   Yellow decorating sugar (optional)

Beat butter in large bowl with electric mixer at medium speed until smooth. Add sugar; beat until well blended. Add egg, lemon juice and peel; beat until well blended.

Combine flour, baking powder, salt and nutmeg in large bowl. Gradually add flour mixture to butter mixture at low speed, blending well after each addition.

Shape dough into 2 logs, each about 1½ inches in diameter and 6½ inches long. Roll logs in yellow sugar, if desired. Wrap each log in plastic wrap. Refrigerate 2 to 3 hours or up to 3 days.

Preheat oven to 350°F. Grease cookie sheets. Cut logs into ¼-inch-thick slices; place 1 inch apart on cookie sheets.

Bake about 15 minutes or until edges are light brown. Transfer to wire racks to cool. Store in airtight container.

nutrients per serving (1 cookie): 54 Calories, 8g Carbohydrate, <1g Dietary Fiber, 2g Total Fat, 1g Saturated Fat, 10mg Cholesterol, 32mg Sodium, 1g Protein

Lip-Smacking Lemon Cookies

Spiced Wafers

Makes about 4 dozen cookies

½ cup (1 stick) butter, softened
1 cup sugar
1 egg
2 tablespoons milk
1 teaspoon vanilla
1¾ cups all-purpose flour
2 teaspoons baking powder
1 teaspoon ground cinnamon
½ teaspoon ground nutmeg
¼ teaspoon ground cloves
    Red hot candies or red colored sugar for garnish (optional)

Beat butter in large bowl with electric mixer at medium speed until smooth. Add sugar; beat until well blended. Add egg, milk and vanilla; beat until well blended.

Combine flour, baking powder, cinnamon, nutmeg and cloves in large bowl. Gradually add flour mixture to butter mixture at low speed, blending well after each addition.

Shape dough into 2 logs, each about 2 inches in diameter and 6 inches long. Wrap each log in plastic wrap. Refrigerate 2 to 3 hours or overnight.

Preheat oven to 350°F. Grease cookie sheets. Cut logs into ¼-inch-thick slices; decorate with candies or colored sugar, if desired. Place at least 2 inches apart on cookie sheets.

Bake 11 to 13 minutes or until edges are light brown. Transfer to wire racks to cool. Store in airtight container.

nutrients per serving (1 cookie): 52 Calories, 8g Carbohydrate, <1g Dietary Fiber, 2g Total Fat, 1g Saturated Fat, 10mg Cholesterol, 37mg Sodium, 1g Protein

Spiced Wafers

Chocolate Chip Cookies

Makes about 2 dozen cookies

⅓ cup stick butter or margarine, softened
1 egg
1 teaspoon vanilla
⅓ cup EQUAL® SPOONFUL*
⅓ cup firmly packed light brown sugar
¾ cup all-purpose flour
½ teaspoon baking soda
¼ teaspoon salt
½ cup semi-sweet chocolate chips or mini chocolate chips

May substitute 8 packets Equal® sweetener.

• Beat butter with electric mixer until fluffy. Beat in egg and vanilla until blended. Mix in Equal® and brown sugar until combined.

• Combine flour, baking soda and salt. Mix into butter mixture until well blended. Stir in chocolate chips.

• Drop dough by rounded teaspoonfuls onto ungreased baking sheet. Bake in preheated 350°F oven 8 to 10 minutes or until light golden color. Remove from baking sheet and cool completely on wire rack.

nutrients per serving (1 cookie): 70 Calories, 9g Carbohydrate, <1g Dietary Fiber, 4g Total Fat, 2g Saturated Fat, 16mg Cholesterol, 74mg Sodium, 1g Protein

Chocolate Chip Cookies

Butterscotch Crispies

Makes 8½ dozen cookies

2 cups sifted all-purpose flour
1 teaspoon baking soda
1 teaspoon salt
½ cup margarine
2½ cups packed light brown sugar
2 eggs
1 teaspoon vanilla extract
2 cups quick-cooking rolled oats
2 cups puffed rice cereal
½ cup chopped walnuts

Preheat oven to 350°F. Sift flour, baking soda and salt onto waxed paper. Cream margarine and brown sugar with electric mixer at medium speed in large bowl until fluffy. Beat in eggs, 1 at a time, until fluffy. Stir in vanilla.

Add flour mixture, ⅓ at a time, until well blended; stir in rolled oats, rice cereal and walnuts. Drop by teaspoonfuls, about 1 inch apart, onto large cookie sheets lightly sprayed with nonstick cooking spray. Bake 10 minutes or until cookies are firm and lightly golden. Remove to wire racks; cool.

Favorite recipe from **The Sugar Association, Inc.**

nutrients per serving (1 cookie): 50 Calories, 9g Carbohydrate, <1g Dietary Fiber, 1g Total Fat, <1g Saturated Fat, 4mg Cholesterol, 49mg Sodium, 1g Protein

Butterscotch Crispies

Macadamia Nut Crunchies

Makes 2 dozen cookies

½ cup mashed ripe banana (about 2 medium bananas)
⅓ cup butter or margarine, melted
¼ cup no-sugar-added pineapple fruit spread
1 egg, beaten
1 teaspoon vanilla
1¼ cups all-purpose flour
⅓ cup unsweetened flaked coconut*
½ teaspoon baking powder
½ teaspoon salt
1 jar (3½ ounces) macadamia nuts, coarsely chopped (about ¾ cup)

Unsweetened flaked coconut is available in health food stores.

1. Preheat oven to 375°F. Lightly grease cookie sheets.

2. Combine banana, melted butter, fruit spread, egg and vanilla in medium bowl. Add flour, coconut, baking powder and salt; mix well. Stir in nuts. Drop tablespoonfuls of dough 2 inches apart onto prepared cookie sheets.

3. Bake 10 to 12 minutes or until lightly browned. Cool on wire racks. Store in tightly covered container.

nutrients per serving (1 cookie): 101 Calories, 10g Carbohydrate, 1g Dietary Fiber, 6g Total Fat, 3g Saturated Fat, 16mg Cholesterol, 89mg Sodium, 1g Protein

Macadamia Nut Crunchies

Peanut Butter Chocolate Bars

Makes 4 dozen bars

1 cup EQUAL® SPOONFUL*
½ cup (1 stick) butter or margarine, softened
⅓ cup firmly packed brown sugar
½ cup 2% milk
½ cup creamy peanut butter
1 egg
1 teaspoon vanilla
1 cup all-purpose flour
1 cup quick oats, uncooked
½ teaspoon baking soda
¼ teaspoon salt
¾ cup mini semi-sweet chocolate chips

May substitute 24 packets Equal® sweetener.

• Beat Equal®, butter and brown sugar until well combined. Stir in milk, peanut butter, egg and vanilla until blended. Gradually mix in combined flour, oats, baking soda and salt until blended. Stir in chocolate chips.

• Spread mixture evenly in 13×9-inch baking pan generously coated with nonstick cooking spray. Bake in preheated 350°F oven 20 to 22 minutes. Cool completely in pan on wire rack. Cut into squares; store in airtight container at room temperature.

nutrients per serving (1 bar): 75 Calories,
8g Carbohydrate, 1g Dietary Fiber, 5g Total Fat, 2g Saturated Fat, 10mg Cholesterol, 60mg Sodium, 1g Protein

Peanut Butter Chocolate Bars

Oatmeal Almond Balls

Makes 2 dozen cookies

¼ cup sliced almonds
2 egg whites
⅓ cup honey
½ teaspoon ground cinnamon
⅛ teaspoon salt
1½ cups uncooked quick oats

1. Preheat oven to 350°F. Place almonds on ungreased cookie sheet; bake 8 to 10 minutes or until golden brown. Set aside. Do not turn off oven.

2. Combine egg whites, honey, cinnamon and salt in large bowl; stir until well blended. Add oats and toasted almonds; stir until well blended. Drop dough by rounded teaspoonfuls onto ungreased nonstick cookie sheets.

3. Bake 12 minutes or until lightly browned. Remove to wire racks; cool completely.

> *nutrients per serving (1 cookie):* 42 Calories, 7g Carbohydrate, 0g Dietary Fiber, 1g Total Fat, 0g Saturated Fat, 0mg Cholesterol, 16mg Sodium, 1g Protein

Oatmeal Almond Balls

Pumpkin Polka Dot Cookies

Makes about 4 dozen cookies

1¼ cups EQUAL® SPOONFUL*
½ cup stick butter or margarine, softened
3 tablespoons light molasses
1 cup canned pumpkin
1 egg
1½ teaspoons vanilla
1⅔ cups all-purpose flour
1 teaspoon baking powder
1¼ teaspoons ground cinnamon
½ teaspoon ground nutmeg
½ teaspoon ground ginger
½ teaspoon baking soda
¼ teaspoon salt
1 cup mini semi-sweet chocolate chips

May substitute 30 packets Equal® sweetener.

• Beat Equal®, butter and molasses until well combined. Mix in pumpkin, egg and vanilla until blended. Gradually stir in combined flour, baking powder, spices, baking soda and salt until well blended. Stir in chocolate chips.

• Drop by teaspoonfuls onto baking sheet sprayed with nonstick cooking spray. Bake in preheated 350°F oven 11 to 13 minutes. Remove from baking sheet and cool completely on wire rack. Store at room temperature in airtight container up to 1 week.

nutrients per serving (1 cookie): 63 Calories,
8g Carbohydrate, 1g Dietary Fiber, 3g Total Fat, 2g Saturated Fat,
10mg Cholesterol, 69mg Sodium, 1g Protein

Pumpkin Polka Dot Cookies

Double Chocolate Brownies

Makes 16 servings

¾ cup all-purpose flour
1 cup EQUAL® SPOONFUL*
½ cup semi-sweet chocolate chips or mini chocolate chips
6 tablespoons unsweetened cocoa
1 teaspoon baking powder
¼ teaspoon salt
6 tablespoons stick butter or margarine, softened
½ cup unsweetened applesauce
2 eggs
1 teaspoon vanilla

May substitute 24 packets Equal® sweetener.

• Combine flour, Equal®, chocolate chips, cocoa, baking powder and salt. Beat butter, applesauce, eggs and vanilla until blended. Stir in combined flour mixture until blended.

• Spread batter in 8-inch square baking pan sprayed with nonstick cooking spray. Bake in preheated 350°F oven 18 to 20 minutes or until top springs back when gently touched. Cool completely on wire rack.

nutrients per serving (1 brownie (¹/₁₆ of total recipe)): **108 Calories, 10g Carbohydrate, 1g Dietary Fiber, 7g Total Fat, 4g Saturated Fat, 38mg Cholesterol, 119mg Sodium, 2g Protein**

Double Chocolate Brownies

Sweet as Angels' Kisses

Makes 5 dozen cookies

4 egg whites, at room temperature
¼ teaspoon cream of tartar
⅛ teaspoon salt
1 cup granulated sugar
¼ teaspoon peppermint or mint extract or desired fruit-flavored
    flavoring
Few drops red or green food coloring
Sprinkles or colored sugar (optional)

1. Preheat oven to 250°F. Line baking sheets with parchment paper or aluminum foil; set aside.

2. Beat egg whites in large bowl with electric mixer at high speed until foamy. Add cream of tartar and salt; beat until soft peaks form. Gradually add sugar, beating until stiff peaks form. Beat in extract and food coloring.

3. Drop rounded tablespoonfuls of egg white mixture onto prepared baking sheets; decorate with sprinkles, if desired.

4. Bake 35 to 45 minutes or until cookies are firm to the touch and just beginning to brown around edges. Remove to wire racks; cool completely.

nutrients per serving (3 cookies): **42 Calories, 10g Carbohydrate, 0g Dietary Fiber, 0g Total Fat, 0g Saturated Fat, 0mg Cholesterol, 26mg Sodium, <1g Protein**

Sweet as Angels' Kisses

Buttery Almond Cookies

Makes about 3½ dozen cookies

1¼ cups all-purpose flour
½ teaspoon baking powder
⅛ teaspoon salt
10 tablespoons butter, softened
¾ cup sugar
1 egg
1 teaspoon vanilla
¾ cup slivered almonds, finely chopped
½ cup slivered almonds (optional)

Preheat oven to 350°F. Grease cookie sheets. Combine flour, baking powder and salt in small bowl.

Beat butter in large bowl with electric mixer at medium speed until smooth. Gradually beat in sugar until blended. Increase speed to high; beat until light and fluffy. Beat in egg until fluffy. Beat in vanilla until blended. Stir in flour mixture until blended. Stir in chopped almonds just until combined.

Drop rounded teaspoonfuls of dough about 2 inches apart onto prepared cookie sheets. Press several slivered almonds into dough of each cookie, if desired.

Bake 12 minutes or until edges are golden brown. Let cookies stand on cookie sheets 5 minutes; transfer to wire racks to cool completely. Store in airtight container.

nutrients per serving (1 cookie): 68 Calories, 7g Carbohydrate, <1g Dietary Fiber, 4g Total Fat, 2g Saturated Fat, 13mg Cholesterol, 35mg Sodium, 1g Protein

Buttery Almond Cookies

Cocoa Nutty Bites

Makes 2 dozen cookies

1 cup creamy unsweetened natural peanut butter*
½ cup light brown sugar, not packed
¼ cup sucralose-based sugar substitute
1 tablespoon unsweetened cocoa powder
½ teaspoon ground cinnamon
¼ teaspoon salt
¼ teaspoon ground ginger
1 egg, beaten

Choose natural peanut butter that is not hydrogenated. Check label carefully.

1. Preheat oven to 350°F. Combine peanut butter, brown sugar, sugar substitute, cocoa, cinnamon, salt and ginger in medium bowl. Add egg; stir until well blended.

2. Shape dough into 24 (1-inch) balls. Place on ungreased cookie sheets. Flatten balls with fork to ½-inch thickness.

3. Bake 10 to 12 minutes or until cookies are firm and lightly browned. Cool on cookie sheets 5 minutes. Remove to wire racks; cool completely.

nutrients per serving (1 cookie): 85 Calories, 8g Carbohydrate, 1g Dietary Fiber, 5g Total Fat, 1g Saturated Fat, 9mg Cholesterol, 79mg Sodium, 3g Protein

Cocoa Nutty Bites

acknowledgments

The publisher would like to thank the companies and organizations listed below for the use of their recipes and photographs in this publication.

Birds Eye® Foods

California Tree Fruit Agreement

CanolaInfo.

ConAgra Foods®

Delmarva Poultry Industry, Inc.

Del Monte Corporation

Egg Beaters®

Equal® sweetener

Guiltless Gourmet®

Hershey Foods Corporation

Hillshire Farm®

McIlhenny Company (TABASCO® brand Pepper Sauce)

Minnesota Cultivated Wild Rice Council

Mrs. Dash®

The J.M. Smucker Company

SPLENDA® is a trademark of McNeil PPC, Inc.

The Sugar Association, Inc.

Reprinted with permission of Sunkist Growers, Inc.

Unilever Bestfoods North America

index

METRIC CONVERSION CHART

VOLUME MEASUREMENTS (dry)

$1/8$ teaspoon = 0.5 mL
$1/4$ teaspoon = 1 mL
$1/2$ teaspoon = 2 mL
$3/4$ teaspoon = 4 mL
1 teaspoon = 5 mL
1 tablespoon = 15 mL
2 tablespoons = 30 mL
$1/4$ cup = 60 mL
$1/3$ cup = 75 mL
$1/2$ cup = 125 mL
$2/3$ cup = 150 mL
$3/4$ cup = 175 mL
1 cup = 250 mL
2 cups = 1 pint = 500 mL
3 cups = 750 mL
4 cups = 1 quart = 1 L

VOLUME MEASUREMENTS (fluid)

1 fluid ounce (2 tablespoons) = 30 mL
4 fluid ounces ($1/2$ cup) = 125 mL
8 fluid ounces (1 cup) = 250 mL
12 fluid ounces ($1 1/2$ cups) = 375 mL
16 fluid ounces (2 cups) = 500 mL

WEIGHTS (mass)

$1/2$ ounce = 15 g
1 ounce = 30 g
3 ounces = 90 g
4 ounces = 120 g
8 ounces = 225 g
10 ounces = 285 g
12 ounces = 360 g
16 ounces = 1 pound = 450 g

DIMENSIONS

$1/16$ inch = 2 mm
$1/8$ inch = 3 mm
$1/4$ inch = 6 mm
$1/2$ inch = 1.5 cm
$3/4$ inch = 2 cm
1 inch = 2.5 cm

OVEN TEMPERATURES

250°F = 120°C
275°F = 140°C
300°F = 150°C
325°F = 160°C
350°F = 180°C
375°F = 190°C
400°F = 200°C
425°F = 220°C
450°F = 230°C

BAKING PAN SIZES

Utensil	Size in Inches/Quarts	Metric Volume	Size in Centimeters
Baking or	$8 \times 8 \times 2$	2 L	$20 \times 20 \times 5$
Cake Pan	$9 \times 9 \times 2$	2.5 L	$23 \times 23 \times 5$
(square or	$12 \times 8 \times 2$	3 L	$30 \times 20 \times 5$
rectangular)	$13 \times 9 \times 2$	3.5 L	$33 \times 23 \times 5$
Loaf Pan	$8 \times 4 \times 3$	1.5 L	$20 \times 10 \times 7$
	$9 \times 5 \times 3$	2 L	$23 \times 13 \times 7$
Round Layer	$8 \times 1 1/2$	1.2 L	20×4
Cake Pan	$9 \times 1 1/2$	1.5 L	23×4
Pie Plate	$8 \times 1 1/4$	750 mL	20×3
	$9 \times 1 1/4$	1 L	23×3
Baking Dish	1 quart	1 L	—
or Casserole	$1 1/2$ quart	1.5 L	—
	2 quart	2 L	—